A Lawyer's CASE for GOD

A Lawyer's CASE for GOD

Jim Jacob, Esq.

Yaakov press

About the Author

Since 1979 Jim Jacob has been engaged in the practice of law and has been a senior partner at his law firm. Jim holds the highest rating from a prominent company that evaluates lawyers nationwide. He has been privileged to represent civic leaders, large U.S. companies, and individuals. Jim is admitted to practice before the U.S. Supreme Court. He was selected for membership by Outstanding Lawyers of America. A major metropolitan newspaper requested him to author a series of articles on legal topics. He also has authored articles for a statewide legal publication. Jim has been married for 28 years and has four children. He and his wife Cathy have served as leaders at their congregation for many years.

Acknowledgment

I would like to thank my beloved wife Cathy for her prayers and love throughout our 28 years of marriage. I have been blessed beyond measure with a woman who far surpasses my dreams. Without her patience and kindness, this book would not have been possible. Her heartfelt input and prayers were extremely beneficial.

I also thank my children who have prayed for me, inspired me over the years, and assisted with this endeavor. They are a tremendous blessing. I am also grateful to Don and Jackie Goldstein, Marvin Aaron, Shmuel Wolkenfeld, Jack and Liz Kaufman, David Belpedio, and others who also assisted with this book.

Lastly, I would like to thank God for His protection, patience, and everlasting love.

Introduction

My anti-religious views and the reason for this book

I Was a Committed Atheist for 39 Years

For the majority of my life I was a deeply committed atheist, absolutely certain there was no God. I was confident that God was created in the minds of naive human beings to answer questions they could not. God was a myth that provided nothing more than false hope. I was certain that these crazy Christians, religious Jews, and other religious fanatics were totally deceived and were hooked on religion, like drug addicts were hooked on drugs.

I was convinced the Bible was simply made up to give us a reason to tolerate all the rotten things in the world like pain, suffering, death, taxes, and more taxes, not to mention wasteful government spending and virtually non-stop political advertising. Gullible people simply clung to the hope that everything would be better once they endured the travails of life on earth and entered paradise in heaven.

I was raised in a Jewish home, but must admit that I thought Abraham, Isaac, Jacob, Noah, Moses, and the rest of the supporting biblical cast were nothing more than fictional characters, akin to Rumpelstiltskin, Cinderella, and Hansel and Gretel. Anyone with a lick of sense could see right through the fairy tales in the Bible.

To me, spending time and energy on religion was an utter waste of time. My attitude closely resembled the sentiments expressed by Bill Gates: "...religion is not very efficient. There is a lot more I could do on Sunday morning."[1]

I was totally convinced my views were correct and that all the rules religious fanatics (I thought all religious people were fanatics) walked in lock step with were insane and, in fact, almost comical. It grieved me that people squandered money on church buildings, mosques, and synagogues. I could not understand why anyone would pray or live a "holy" life. How unnecessary! How boring! If it worked for them that was fine, but it was definitely not for me and never would be...or so I thought.

Of course, I had arrived at these steadfast convictions without examining *any* of the facts. I just somehow, almost supernaturally, by osmosis felt that religion was all wrong. The closest I had even come to reading the Bible was scanning the 23rd Psalm on a record-store poster.

"Don't talk religion with friends," is a well-known creed, and I clung to it. Had I not embraced that axiom, I might have realized that I was not simply *misinformed*—I was totally *uninformed*. Now that I have studied and pondered these issues, I realize my previous opinions had no factual or rational basis whatsoever. I had actually established my own rules and thus had essentially created my own religion in which I was the sole congregant.

In hindsight, what I find so amazing is that I had virtually ignored such an important topic. What if I was wrong? The consequences were extreme—eternity lasts a long time!

In this book, I will respond to many of my own former opinions. In fact, that is why I have written this book: to illuminate some evidence and apply simple logic to issues pertaining to the existence of God, validity of the Bible, and purpose of life. Each chapter addresses a position I previously held and offers analysis for your consideration.

Decisions about God, of course, are yours to make. I simply offer the kind of information I wish I had explored many years earlier. The chapters build upon one another, so I encourage you to read them in order and consider them with an open mind. You may wish to say a short prayer right now asking God, if He is real, to open your heart and reveal Himself to you.

Chapter 1

Argument
Religion is a waste of time and not for me

It's Your Decision

Many proclaim "religion may work for some people, and I am happy for them, but to me, religion is a total waste of time." If you feel this way, you certainly are not alone. As noted in the Introduction, you are in the company of Bill Gates who apparently feels the same. But are you correct? Have you sufficiently addressed this important decision?

Fortunately, in a free society, we are allowed to make our own decisions about God, religion, and countless other matters. We are free to decide whom to marry, where to live, what to do for a living, and so on. Typically, before making a decision that will significantly impact our well-being, we very carefully consider the options. The more important the matter, the more we tend to scrutinize the situation.

The Decision-Making Process

In making decisions, we weigh the pros and cons and then make a choice. Sometimes we believe we have it all figured out, only to learn later that we miscalculated. The puppy that seemed so cute curled up next to his mama can turn out to be a terror who thinks your furniture is his chew stick and your carpet his potty. Society has even coined a term for this change of heart—"buyer's remorse."

The more important the matter, the more we tend to explore and inquire. Before choosing a spouse, we typically investigate quite extensively. Some even choose to live with a potential mate for a while, before closing the deal and saying "I do"...or "I don't." Many of us do extensive background checks before even going out on a first date, as we know the wrong choice in that area can result in a challenging evening.

Decisions Regarding the Afterlife...
Is There a More Significant Decision?

Many believe that there is an afterlife. Others disagree. I cannot think of a decision with more upside or downside potential, can you? What else comes even close? New car? Sell it if you make the wrong choice. Wrong job? Quit. Wrong spouse? That can have long-lasting effects, but worst-case scenario—75 years of aggravation with reprieves when you sleep, go to work, or engage in other distractions.

It seems that the issue of whether there is life after death is such a crucial matter that it warrants a thorough investigation, carried out with utmost care, leaving no stone unturned. Yet many of us give this subject little thought. I shunned those who wanted to talk about it. I steered clear of people I felt were "holy rollers." Some of these individuals were a little hard to take (OK, very hard to take), and might benefit from a few more semesters at God U. or Spread-the-Word College. But was it prudent to reject the *message*, merely because the *messenger* was annoying?

Before concluding that things of God are a waste of time and not for you, I urge you to read on and ponder some evidence that I did not know when I held a similar position. Let's follow the evidence and see where it leads. (And I will try not to be too annoying!)

Chapter 2

Argument
There is no evidence that God exists

Imagine you are walking along a sandy beach and you stumble upon a robot. Would you conclude that someone had assembled the robot and left it there? Or would you decide that this robot had assembled by random chance? It would clearly take a quantum leap of faith to conclude that the robot just happened by chance, even if the robot had many years to assemble.

Now let's compare a robot to a human being. I think we can all agree that there is absolutely no comparison. Although a robot is remarkable and many have dreamt of having one to order around, human beings are far more complex and are undoubtedly the most amazing "machine" ever.

How did humans get here? Did God create us? To help answer these questions, let's briefly and simplistically examine some of the intricacies and complexities of the human body.

Your Brain

You have a brain that analyzes, recalls, calculates, communicates, comprehends, and operates your entire body. No computer can come close to that. Your brain even equips you with the ability to accept or reject the existence of God. Your brain can instantaneously send messages to your tongue, mouth, and lips, instructing them precisely how to contort so you can effortlessly verbalize a word that someone else can comprehend—thanks to his or her own brain!

Do you want to see the amazing versatility and capabilities of a simple part of your body? Please open and close your fist. How did that happen? Your brain sent a signal to your hand instructing it to behave as you desired. Your brain did not have to physically touch your hand to make it move. Instead, it sent an electrical signal through your nerves (biological electrical cables) and spinal cord to the muscles in your hand and voilà, the clench of your fist, the snap of your fingers, or the creation of art. The options and features are only limited by the creativity of your brain. Your hand also collects sensory information, such as touch and temperature, which it sends to your spinal cord and back to your brain for processing.[2] Your hand has more standard features than a brand new Mercedes! Sir Isaac Newton, a brilliant discerning scientist, concluded "the thumb alone would convince me of God's existence."[3]

While you sleep, fortunately your brain does not shut down. Instead, it continues to work and keep you alive. It also allows you to dream. You can dream some rather bizarre scenarios that might include talking trees, flying pizza, mammoth scoops of ice cream, and horses in the shape of wagons. These remarkable "special effects" are produced by your incredible brain!

After a full night of dreaming, you typically awake refreshed. This replenishing feature is incorporated right into your body. Do you know another machine that recharges itself…on its own?

Your brain commands your legs to walk, run, or ride a bike with ease, and even enables your body to multi-task. Many of us can converse with someone about a complex topic while driving a car or putting away groceries.

When your brain is in conscious-mode, it can remember details of birthdays and other special events and occurrences for 80 years or more! I can vividly remember events that happened when I was a young child and most likely you can too. Your brain also has memory that enables you to effortlessly recall a commercial jingle or hit song you have not heard for decades! The capabilities of your brain are something to behold!

Your Eyes

While you were relaxing peacefully in your mother's womb, over *one million* nerve fibers from your brain each matched up flawlessly with the correct stations in your retina and your vision was established.[4] Imagine the likelihood of that occurrence!

The moment you were born, your eyes began "e-mailing" three dimensional digital images to your brain that were, most likely, perfectly in focus. Throughout your lifetime, your eyelids have instinctively blinked to provide moisture that is essential to the function of your eyeballs. Imagine the challenge it would be to sleep without eyelids.

For optimal performance, the pupil of your eye gradually contracts when it is bright and sunny and dilates when it is dark. Variations in these automatic setting options for your pupils are virtually infinite.

Some eyes even change color in the sun. The standard features on your eyes are extraordinary. Your eye is a highly sophisticated and technologically advanced piece of equipment. Did your eyes just happen by chance or did they have a designer?

Even Charles Darwin, the creator of the theory of evolution, acknowledged that it was "absurd in the highest degree" to conclude that the eye happened by chance:

> To suppose that the eye with all its inimitable contrivances for adjusting the focus to different distances, for admitting different amounts of light, and for the correction of spherical and chromatic aberration, could have been formed by natural selection, seems, I freely confess, absurd in the highest degree.[5]

Your Digestive System

In simple, non-graphic terms, your digestive system includes four component parts: mouth, throat, stomach, and intestines. You could not survive without any of the four; they all had to appear on the scene simultaneously. Essentially a complete and highly sophisticated assembly line exists inside of you!

The assembly line begins with your mouth where teeth tear and grind up food so it can travel down your throat. You do not even have to think about swallowing. It has been virtually automatic since you were an infant. Just before swallowing you are afforded the opportunity to savor the flavor of the food courtesy of about 200 taste buds on your tongue.[6] After swallowing, your body inexplicably creates and secretes the precise chemicals needed, at the appropriate spots, to further break down the food. This assembly line performs all necessary tasks as the food travels on to its next destination. Nothing is out of order. All is perfectly fine-tuned. Numerous parts work in perfect harmony with each other; among these are the tongue, salivary glands, pharynx, esophagus, sphincters, stomach, small intestine, liver, gall bladder, pancreas, and large intestine.[7]

At the end of the assembly line, nourishment is distributed throughout your body—to your muscles, skin, and other tissues. Most of what is not needed is eliminated. If this elimination phase in the digestive process did not happen, you would explode or be poisoned. Simply amazing, is it not, that all of these components are perfectly placed? It is difficult for me to believe that this highly sophisticated system randomly assembled.

Your Heart and Circulatory System

You are equipped with a heart, with four distinct chambers, which pumps vitally needed oxygen-rich blood to each of the 75 trillion cells in your body. This is done 24/7 without any conscious effort on your part. Your body is capable of replenishing its blood and the blood itself is capable of distributing oxygen throughout your body. Your blood is also able to clot. Without this "special effect," most of us would die after our first shave, if not sooner.

To transport blood, your heart requires *75,000 miles* of intricately woven blood vessels. You have three types of blood vessels (veins, arteries, and capillaries) which are anatomically distinct and perform different functions. Arteries are elastic; they expand and contract as they pump the blood *away* from your heart. Veins return the blood *back* to your heart and contain strategically placed valves which prevent blood from pooling and flowing back to your legs due to gravity. Capillaries are merely one cell in diameter and perform various functions depending upon where they are placed in the body.[8]

Imagine if all of these components did not materialize at the same time! I cannot imagine the blueprints or engineering expertise required for such an intricate system. Can you?

Your Body

Is this "machine" brought to you by random chance or by an almighty God who had the power and ingenuity to create the most amazing machine ever? King David, of David-and-Goliath fame and one of Israel's greatest kings, credited God for our bodies:

> I will praise You [God] for I am fearfully and wonderfully made. *Psalm 139:14*

Was King David correct? Let's ponder that further by briefly examining the miracle of conception and childbirth as well as other features of our bodies.

At conception, two microscopic cells join together and continuously multiply *billions* of times until a fully functioning human being is formed. The unborn child survives in a womb without air until suddenly, after passing through the birth canal, it begins breathing through developed lungs. This life-saving procedure is performed by a newborn infant who cannot even crawl or utter a word yet! Another vital feature is built into the mother—she starts producing milk at just the right moment and then stops...until her next child is born.

This newborn develops into a "machine" that has the ability to create other machines. I know of no other machine with that capability. My lawn-mower cannot do that; my car cannot do that; my remote control cannot do that; even my computer cannot do that.

Your body, if it is like mine, has been running *non-stop* for a long time. Damaged by cuts, bruises, and broken bones, it repairs itself without any instruction from us! No other machine can do that. In fact, many machines I buy seem to *break*—not *fix*—themselves, but that may just be me.

My wife slipped on ice and fractured her wrist in the winter of 2006. The doctor surgically inserted pins to hold the broken bones together while they healed—on their own. The nurse informed her that her nerves would regenerate and she would feel twinges as her muscles adapted to the situation and re-formed around her new bone. How fascinating that our bodies recognize the traumatic situation and respond accordingly to restore us!

Your body also has certain essential built-in response mechanisms, such as coughing and perspiring. If you did not cough, you would have long since choked to death. If your body was not programmed to perspire, you would have overheated the first time you took a long walk on a warm day.

Your muscles also have "muscle memory." Through simple repetition your muscles unconsciously learn to automatically and precisely repeat certain functions. You learned to walk when you were about a year old and now do so with virtually no conscious effort. Similarly, you can probably ride a bike, drive a car, and type without much thought.

Strategically placed facial muscles allow you to produce a countless array of facial expressions displaying joy, sorrow, anger, and surprise. These expressions, and the emotions they reveal, are instinctive. You can reveal a great deal about your feelings with a perfectly formed facial expression that is stern, compassionate, guilty, embarrassed, proud, loving, shocked, or flirtatious.

Contemplate these additional intriguing facts about the human body:

- Our DNA carries *3 billion* characters (nucleotides) which establish the code for *every* characteristic and feature in our unique body.[9]

- We have 75 trillion cells and each one carries our DNA.[10]

- If our DNA was unraveled it would reach the moon![11]

- The probability that the average gene would form spontaneously is 1 in $4^{19,000}$—a virtual impossibility![12]

- On the surface of *each* of our 75 trillion cells is one of over 10,000 proteins in our body called laminin. Laminin is a vital adhesion protein that holds our cells together. Without these trillions of laminin proteins our body would fall apart. Every laminin protein is in the shape of a lower case letter "t."[13]

- Our "feeling" sensations are so sensitive we can feel the wing of a bee fall upon our face.[14]

- Our smell sensations are activated through 5 million receptors at the top of each nasal cavity that can differentiate between a freshly baked apple pie and fried chicken. In many, this smell sensation is keen enough to detect a drop of perfume across the room.[15]

- Our hearing can recognize a familiar voice with the uttering of merely one syllable. To hear a sound, the parts of our ear perform an intricate mechanical chain reaction transferring vibrating air to a moving piston to fluid waves to chemical impulses to the brain.[16] (An ear, nose, and throat doctor recently told me that our hearing system is so intricate that doctors do not understand precisely how it functions and that no one has been able to replicate anything even close to it. Is evolution able to randomly produce something far more sophisticated than what can be created by the best and brightest doctors, scientists, and engineers?)

- The simple task of shaking hands requires the precise movement of 200 muscles (most of which are unknown to us) that we instruct based on feedback received simultaneously from our brain and eye as to the position of the other person's hand. Hitting a 70-mph tennis ball or baseball is far more complex, yet our eye-hand coordination can accomplish this as well.[17] Reflect upon the interfacing of the mind, eye, and countless muscles, as a gymnast or ballerina gracefully performs.

We are miracles, are we not?

Programming of Your Body

We do not grow forever—at least vertically. Every person is programmed to attain a certain height. Imagine if you kept getting taller throughout life. You would constantly outgrow your bed, your car, and even your home!

The hair on your head never stops growing, yet eyelashes, eyebrows, and arm hair do. Teeth stop growing. Fingernails do not. How does each body part "know" this?

Instincts in Animals

Animals possess instincts. Instincts are not learned, yet they can be complex and life-saving. Even Charles Darwin expressed concern that instinctive behavior in animals seriously threatened to "overthrow" his theory of evolution:

> Many instincts are so wonderful that their development will probably appear to the reader a difficulty sufficient to overthrow my whole theory.[18]

A few examples of invaluable animal instincts are:

- Geese fly south for the winter in flocks in V-formation.

- Bees and other insects pollinate flowers.

- Beavers build dams to protect their habitat.

- Ants join forces to build intricate underground colonies.

- Salmon swim upstream to spawn.

- Mammals mate and care for their newborn.

- Bears hibernate in the winter.

- Bees extract nectar from flowers to create honey and even perform a unique "dance" for other bees that provides them specific directions to the flower.[19]

The list goes on and on. These animals were not *trained* to do these things—they were *programmed* to do them.

Those Remarkable Single-File Marching Penguins

A very intriguing species is the penguin. I knew virtually nothing about penguins until I saw the documentary *The March of the Penguins*. The filmmaker captures on film thousands of penguins in a remote area of Antarctica suddenly one day climbing out of the frigid ocean water (which their bodies are equipped to withstand), one right after the other, immediately forming an impressive single-file line. Who taught them to line up single-file? It can be quite a challenge to persuade grade school children from our more intelligent species to perform this task. It would even be problematic to convince adults to do this year after year without hearing some complaining. But not one of the penguins even attempts to cut in line.

These penguins then proceed to march (actually it is more of a waddle) single file, non-stop, until they reach their destination approximately 70 miles away—the mating area. No maps; no GPS; yet they arrive at their destination without making one wrong turn. Upon their arrival, all of the penguins instinctively search among the thousands of birds to find a mate. They each choose another penguin for this season with barely any fighting among themselves. Imagine the likelihood of thousands matching up perfectly!

The penguins then know how to mate. Grade school children require sex education classes, or chats with blushing parents, to acquire this knowledge, yet penguins are programmed with the information. After the penguins mate, an egg forms inside the mother and, as if possessing a built-in timer, at precisely the right moment, the egg is expelled into the bone-chilling Antarctic temperatures. The mother somehow senses the importance of keeping the egg warm. After weeks of not eating, the mother treks back to the ocean for food and nourishment, leaving the father to care for the egg. Chaos would have ensued had my wife left me in charge of our newborns, especially in Antarctica. Fortunately, papa penguins are also aware of the need to keep the egg warm while the mama is away.

Additionally, the baby penguins each receive their first food from the mouth of their father. The father, who has not eaten for literally months, is able to regurgitate a partially digested meal reserved just for this moment.

I find this fascinating. The details and timing of these instincts can only be explained by the existence of a creator who designed them.

Evolution

Micro-evolution is accepted by many and I do not dispute it. It simply claims that small changes occur over time within a species, such as a wolf evolving into a dog. Macro-evolution, on the other hand, speculates that all life evolved from a speck of matter, that a single cell evolved into complex cell structures, and that humans evolved from apes. This theory is disputed by many and seems comparable to concluding that the robot evolved on the beach by chance. Also, macro-evolution fails to explain how the first matter got here.

To accept macro-evolution as truth, we have to presume that the original matter did not decay, but rather expanded its horizons and progressed to an amazingly complex human. This is contrary to the Second Law of Thermodynamics, often called the law of entropy, which was viewed by Albert Einstein as the *premier* law of science. The Second Law of Thermodynamics states that things tend to degenerate or decay—metal naturally rusts; rusted metal does not naturally un-rust.

To endorse the theory of macro-evolution, it seems we must also believe that both a male and female gender evolved at precisely the same time in world history and in the exact same place in the world. We also have to believe that our compatible male and female reproductive organs just happened by chance.

Macro-evolution must explain how our incredibly intricate DNA developed. Our bodies are irreducibly complex. Nearly 700 international scientists have expressed their skepticism of macro-evolution and have signed their names to the following:

> We are skeptical of claims for the ability of random mutation and natural selection to account for the complexity of life. Careful examination of the evidence for Darwinian theory should be encouraged.[20]

A similar list of dissenters exists among physicians and surgeons.[21]

Additionally, evolution offers no explanation for the development of our emotions—feelings such as love, hatred, joy, grief, satisfaction, frustration, pride, and guilt. It is baffling to consider that inanimate matter could jump the chasm to engage in complex emotional relationships. How do we explain these emotions if we are just rearranged matter?

This same statistically improbable process had to not only happen with humans, but also with monkeys, dogs, giraffes, cows, and horses, while not accidentally creating cross species such as a half human, half horse. There is no evidence in the fossil record of *any* cross species. With all due respect to Charles Darwin...no way!

In fact, Darwin himself conceded the tenuous nature of his theory of evolution:

> For I am well aware that scarcely a single point is discussed in this volume on which facts cannot be adduced, often apparently leading to conclusions directly opposite to those at which I arrived.[22]

A Reality: Shredded Papers Will Never Reassemble

If you shredded 100 pieces of newspaper, do you think you could ever reassemble them? I cannot imagine ever being able to do this even if I was incredibly bored and had an enormous amount of time and assistance. And if these shredded pages lay dormant for years, what are the chances they would somehow reassemble? In fact, I doubt that one shredded page could even reassemble into one page. If a shredded piece of newspaper could not randomly re-assemble over time, could a human body possibly randomly assemble?

Renowned Individuals Acknowledge a Creator

Albert Einstein, a Nobel Prize winner and professor at Princeton University, and considered by some to be the brightest person who ever lived, acknowledged the existence of a Creator:

> I want to know how God created the world....I want to know His thoughts; the rest are details.[23]

Sir Isaac Newton agreed:

> This most beautiful system of the sun, planets, and comets, could only proceed from the counsel and dominion of an intelligent and powerful Being.[24]

Ralph Waldo Emerson, renowned American author and poet, boldly proclaimed:

> All I have seen has taught me to trust the Creator for all I have not seen.[25]

George Washington Carver, a former slave who became an advisor to world leaders and scientists from Thomas Edison to Mahatma Gandhi, shared his insight into how God communicates with us:

> I love to think of nature as an unlimited broadcasting system, through which God speaks to us every hour, if we will only tune in.[26]

Finally, the drafters of the United States Declaration of Inde-pendence recognized a Creator when they concluded:

> ...all men are created equal, that they are endowed
> by their Creator with certain unalienable Rights,
> that among these are Life, Liberty, and the pursuit of
> Happiness.[27]

Let's shift our focus and briefly overview the expanse, magnitude, order, and balance in our universe that also served as an impetus for these conclusions.

The Universe

The Stars

The expanse of the universe far exceeds our comprehension. Our sun is 93 million miles from earth. The Whirlpool Galaxy is 31 million *light years* away! A light year is 5.88 *trillion* miles. So the Whirlpool Galaxy is 31 million x 5.88 trillion miles away! That is 182.28 *quintillion* miles!

Similarly, the magnitude of the universe surpasses our comprehension. Each galaxy contains billions of stars, and it is estimated there are 130 billion galaxies in our universe![28] After considering the vast multitude of stars in the sky, the psalmist concluded:

> The heavens declare the glory of God.
> *Psalm 19:1*

The largest star discovered to date is Canis Majoris (the Big Dog) which is large enough to hold 7 quadrillion earths! To help you conceptualize this size, mull over that 7 quadrillion seconds is 221,821,300 years! The size of this star is unfathomable to me! If the earth were the size of a golf ball, Canis Majoris could hold enough golf balls to cover the state of Texas...13 times![29]

Is the vast expanse of the universe an awesome display of an awesome God, or did it just happen? The splendor and majesty of the universe seems but a glimpse of the magnificence of its Creator.

Paul Davies, the physicist and Templeton Prize laureate has concluded:

It seems as though somebody has fine-tuned nature's numbers to make the Universe....The impression of design is overwhelming.[30]

A Designer's Fingerprints

The sun has burned brightly for a *long* time. It is located the perfect distance from the earth so we neither freeze nor melt. If the sun were merely .01% closer to the earth, its extreme heat would completely destroy us.

The sun provides another vital function—its light enables plants to grow and provides light to an otherwise dark world. Thank God we have a sun! Try to imagine life without that device. The moon is also located the perfect distance from the earth. A little closer and ocean tides would flood our planet.

Order and Balance

The earth continually revolves around the sun and rotates on its axis, providing us with continual and consistent day-night cycles as well as changing seasons. These cycles have repeated year after year for millennia and sustain our lives. Fruit ripens for harvest and consumption like clockwork each autumn! The 23 degree slant of the earth generates these seasons. The earth's gravitational force prevents us and our belongings from flying into outer space. Where did gravity come from?

The earth contains order and balance. How did it get that way? There is not order in my garage unless I devote some serious time to creating it. Even my sock drawer does not maintain order unless I give it some attention. Mechanisms and structures do not suddenly become orderly unless there is an organizer and designer.

Air

Plants provide humans and other animals with oxygen while we return the favor and provide them carbon dioxide. Neither could survive without the other. If plants had evolved first, they would not have survived and vice versa. For evolution to be an acceptable proposition, plants and animals had to evolve simultaneously in the same part of the world.

Infinity and Eternity

Do space and time go on forever? That seems impossible. But how can there be a beginning and end to time and space? Surely something happened the day before time commenced, and something will happen the day after it ends. Similarly, there must be something beyond the end of the universe. These perplexing mysteries tell me that there are concepts in our world that are beyond the grasp of our human minds.

Not accepting ideas about our world until we understand and agree with them is like refusing to drive a car until we comprehend the intricacies of the internal combustion engine. On the contrary, most of us simply turn the key and drive by faith, trusting in the manufacturer.

Conclusion

Is there proof that God exists? We have considered evidence in our universe that strongly points to a designer. The decision is yours. Louis Pasteur is the father of microbiology. He revolutionized the medical field with vaccines for rabies, anthrax, and chicken cholera, developed the process for the "*Pasteur*ization" of milk, and laid the foundation for the control of tuberculosis, diphtheria, tetanus, and many other diseases. He examined the evidence and rendered a verdict in favor of a Supreme Being:

> The more I study nature, the more I stand amazed at
> the work of the Creator. Science brings men nearer
> to God.[31]

Does this Creator love us and desire to communicate with us? We will explore that in the chapters ahead.

Chapter 3

Argument

There is no evidence that the Bible is true

Facts About the Bible

The Bible was written on three continents over a 1,600-year period by approximately 40 Jewish people from every walk of life.[32] It contains 66 books, originally written in three languages—Hebrew, Aramaic, and Greek. Despite these incredibly diverse origins, the Bible is considered by many scholars to be a masterpiece of unified literature.

While at first glance some of the Bible may seem outdated and inconsistent, upon further reflection many realize that it contains timeless wisdom applicable to our lives today and is congruous when we delve deeper and understand the culture in which it was written and the message being conveyed. Some examples of its timeless wisdom include the following advice:

> Love your neighbor as yourself.
>
> *Leviticus 19:18 (CJB)*

> Let love and faithfulness never leave you.
>
> *Proverbs 3:3 (NIV)*

> Do not devise evil against your neighbor.
>
> *Proverbs 3:29*

> Hear, my children, the instruction of a father.
>
> *Proverbs 4:1*

> Keep your tongue from evil, and your lips from speaking deceit.
>
> *Psalm 34:13*

> A good name is better than precious ointment.
>
> *Ecclesiastes 7:1*

In addition, woven throughout the Bible are themes of mercy, grace, and repentance. It exhorts us to care for orphans and widows, provide for the poor, and extend a helping hand to persons in need. It includes prohibitions against violence, injustice, theft, and homicide.

To explore the origin and authenticity of the Bible we will now examine: 1) the uncanny accuracy of numerous biblical predictions, 2) archaeological discoveries which vouch for the Bible's accuracy, and 3) scientific facts the Bible proclaimed centuries before humankind discovered them.

Perfect Accuracy of Biblical Predictions Concerning Israel

With bulls-eye accuracy, ancient Jewish prophets foretold numerous events in the pages of the Hebrew Scriptures (Old Covenant) about the history of Israel that have all unfolded precisely as written. Not one of the predictions has missed the mark.

Among these predictions that have already come to pass are:

- **The destruction of the Northern Kingdom of Israel in ancient times.**
  This was foretold in *Amos 9:8:* "Behold, the eyes of the Lord God are on the sinful kingdom [Northern Kingdom of Israel], and I will destroy it from the face of the earth."

- **The scattering of the Jewish people among the nations (the Diaspora).**
  This was foretold in *Jeremiah 9:16:* "I will scatter them [the Israelites] also among the gentiles [nations]..." Also see *Deuteronomy 4:27.*

- **The re-establishment of the nation of Israel literally in one day.**
  This occurred when the United Nations approved the establishment of Israel. (Independence was officially declared on May 14, 1948.) This was foretold in *Isaiah 66:8:* "Shall the earth be made to give birth in one day? Or shall a nation be born at once?"

- **The resurrection of Hebrew as an everyday language after being a dead language for almost 2,000 years.**
  No other extinct language has ever been revived. The return of Hebrew as an everyday language in 1948 was foretold in *Zephaniah 3:9:* "For then I will restore to the peoples a pure language..."

- **The re-gathering of the Jewish people to the Land of Israel in 1948.** No other nation has ever re-gathered after being dispersed. This was foretold in *Isaiah 11:12:* "He will set up a banner for the nations, and will assemble the outcasts of Israel, and gather together the dispersed of Judah [Jews] from the four corners of the earth."

- **The Land of Israel prospering under Jewish control.**
  In 1867 Mark Twain described Israel as "a desolate country...a mournful expanse...a desolation."[33] Satellite pictures of the

Mideast today show the entire region to be a barren waste-land except Israel which contains many green and lush areas. This prospering was foretold in *Ezekiel 36:10–35:* "[T]he cities shall be inhabited and the ruins rebuilt....I will...do better for you [Jewish people] than at your beginnings. Then you shall know that I am the Lord....I will give you a new heart and put a new spirit within you; I will take the heart of stone out of your flesh and give you a heart of flesh....And I will multiply the fruit of your trees and increase of your fields, so that you need never again bear the reproach of famine among the nations....So they will say, 'This land that was desolate has become like the garden of Eden;'" Also, see *Amos 9:11, 14, 15.*

The prophet Isaiah predicted something unthinkable—that the desert in Israel would blossom with roses and fruit:

> ...the desert shall rejoice and blossom as the rose...
> *Isaiah 35:1*

> Israel shall blossom and bud, and fill the face of the world with fruit.
> *Isaiah 27:6*

Today Israel is the flower-producing superpower in the Mideast, exporting 1.5 billion roses annually, making it the third leading exporter in the world of roses to the European Union.[34] Additionally, Israel's leading agricultural product is fruit.[35] Since the late 1950s, Israel has also been sharing its agricultural expertise with scores of countries.[36]

The prophet Jeremiah precisely predicted the 70-year Babylonian captivity of Judah (the Southern Kingdom of Israel) that lasted from 586 BCE to 516 BCE:

> Then it will come to pass, when seventy years are completed, that I will punish the king of Babylon and that nation, the land of the Chaldeans, for their iniquity," says the Lord; "and I will make it (the

Babylonian Empire) a perpetual desolation.

Jeremiah 25:11

The prophet Daniel foretold the stunning victory of the Maccabees against the sinister and powerful tyrant, Antiochus Epiphanes, a story commemorated at the Festival of Lights *(Hanukkah)*:

> ...four kingdoms shall arise and...a king shall arise... who understands sinister schemes....He shall destroy fearfully....He shall destroy the mighty, and also the holy people. Through his cunning he shall cause deceit to prosper under his rule....And he shall exalt himself in his heart....But *he shall be broken* without human means.

Daniel 8:22–25
(See also Daniel 11:3–4)

The pinpoint accuracy of these predictions is unfathomable, unless God, who transcends time, language, and location, inspired the words in the Bible. The Hebrew Scriptures confirm that they are the word of the Lord:

> As for God, His way is perfect; the word of the Lord is proven...

2 Samuel 22:31

Many additional biblical prophecies that have been fulfilled will be discussed in Chapter 12.

Archaeological Evidence in Support of the Bible

Despite efforts by atheists and skeptics, most reputable historians and archaeologists would agree that not one shred of credible evidence has been found to refute *any* historical event recorded in the Bible. In fact, the deeper archaeologists dig, the more evidence they unearth to corroborate the Bible. Rabbi Nelson Glueck, a prominent Jewish archaeologist, concluded that archaeological discoveries have repeatedly affirmed the validity of the Bible:

> ...it may be stated categorically that no archaeological discovery has ever controverted a biblical reference. Scores of archaeological findings have been made which confirm in clear outline or in exact detail historical statements in the Bible. And, by the same token, proper evaluation of biblical descriptions has often led to amazing discoveries. They form tesserae in the vast mosaic of the Bible's almost incredibly correct historical memory.[37]

Some examples of archaeological discoveries which authenticate events recorded in the Bible are:

- **Second Temple**
  The Western or Wailing Wall, a place where people come to pray in Jerusalem today, is actually a portion of the retaining wall for the Second Temple which is discussed extensively in the Bible. Additionally, in 1985 excavations uncovered a 900-foot tunnel by the Western Wall that unmistakably was the style utilized by King Herod who constructed the Second Temple. Tourists to Jerusalem can stroll through this tunnel today at which time they will also see the Warren Gate, one of the ancient gates to the Second Temple.[38] In 2007 an ancient quarry where King Herod's workers chiseled huge high-quality limestone for the construction of the Second Temple was uncovered in Jerusalem.[39]

- **Hezekiah's Tunnel**
  King Hezekiah's tunnel (see *2 Chronicles 32*), which was constructed in 700 BCE to transport water, has been discovered and can be waded through today on a visit to Jerusalem.[40]

- **Sodom and Gomorrah**
  The ruins of Sodom and Gomorrah have been discovered. The Bible records that these cities were destroyed due to their sin.[41] *(Genesis 18–19)*

- **First Temple**
  Evidence of a third gate to King Solomon's Temple was discovered in 1971. The Bible records that King Solomon's Temple was the First Temple constructed in Jerusalem.[42] *(1 Kings 5–6)*

- **Baruch Seals**
  In 1982 archaeologists unearthed 51 clay seals (bullae) of Baruch, scribe and devoted friend of the prophet Jeremiah. One of the seals contained the name Gemariah and was discovered in the precise location in Gemariah's home where *Jeremiah 36:10* records that these parchments were read by Baruch 2,500 years ago.[43]

- **Tombs of Abraham and Sarah and their Family**
  Genesis 23:8–20, 25:9, and *49:30* record that Abraham bought a tomb in Machpelah for his family after the death of his wife Sarah. Abraham and Sarah, as well as their son Isaac and grandson Jacob (and their wives), were buried there. This tomb containing their remains can be viewed in Machpelah today.[44]

- **House of David Inscription**
  Relics unearthed from the ancient City of David in 1993 confirm that King David lived precisely when and where the Bible reports he lived. A piece of basalt containing the inscription "House of David" was discovered by Professor Avraham Biran, director of the Nelson Glueck School of Biblical Archaeology of the Hebrew Union College. Pottery found in the vicinity seems to confirm that the inscription was made just after King David died in the 9th century BCE. Dr. Hershel Shanks of *Biblical Archaeological Review* states, "The stele brings to life the biblical text in a very dramatic way. It also gives us more confidence in the historical reality of the biblical text."[45]

Archaeologists have uncovered evidence confirming the biblical accounts of the life of Joseph, the lives of kings and prophets, and the fallen walls of Jericho.[46] The ancient stones in Israel indeed cry out and speak to us just as God said they would:

> For the stone will cry out from the wall.
>
> *Habakkuk 2:11*

The Stones Cry Out, by Randall Price, as well as the highly respected magazine *Biblical Archaeological Review* contain additional archaeological evidence that confirms the authenticity of the Bible.

Perhaps William Foxwell Albright, American Dean of Biblical Archaeology, summed it up best:

> Discovery after discovery has established the accuracy of innumerable details, and has brought increased recognition of the Bible as a source of history.[47]

Would the Bible contain all of these verifiably true stories, yet contain fiction in other chapters?

The Smithsonian Institution's Department of Anthropology, a secular institution, has acknowledged that "much of the Bible, in particular the historical books of the old testament, are as accurate historical documents as any we have from antiquity and are in fact more accurate than many of the Egyptian, Mesopotamian or Greek histories."[48]

The evidence for the truth of the Bible continues to grow as modern archaeological discoveries continue to validate it. The accidental discovery of the Dead Sea Scrolls in Qumran, near the Dead Sea, which made front-page news in the middle of the 20th century, confirmed the reliability of Scripture for many scholars. The Dead Sea Scrolls were written approximately 1,000 years before the earliest known manuscripts of the Hebrew Scriptures at the time, yet they are virtually identical to each other. The Dead Sea Scrolls confirm the authenticity of current-day translations of the Bible.

William Foxwell Albright hailed the Dead Sea Scrolls as "the greatest manuscript discovery of modern times."[49] If the Bible were a fraud and not actually the inspired word of God, one would expect significant discrepancies between versions written so many years apart. A mere product of human invention would assuredly contain error and bias. In fact, the opposite has proved true—the earlier translations vouch for the accuracy of the later manuscripts.

When these facts are examined together with archaeological evidence, it becomes clear that the Bible is an accurate account of historical events. Regrettably, I was unaware of these facts for the first 39 years of my life when I thought the Bible was a collection of myths and legends.

The Hebrew Scriptures Report Scientific Facts Unknown at the Time by Human Beings

Did you know that the Bible contains numerous scientific facts unknown to humankind at the time they were written? It is true! How could the writers repeatedly foreknow this information unless God imparted it to them? Below are a few examples of this scientific foreknowledge.

The Earth is Round and Suspended in Space

We all know that before 1492 the earth was believed to be flat. This opinion was commonly held about 2,700 years ago when the prophet Isaiah defied conventional wisdom and wrote:

> It is He who sits above the circle of the earth...
>
> *Isaiah 40:22*

About that same time, Job also described the earth as suspended in space.

> He hangs the earth on nothing.
>
> *Job 26:7*

Neither of these facts was known by scientists at the time they were written. Yet, Isaiah and Job knew the truth.

Paths of the Sea

Psalm 8:8, written by King David some 3,000 years ago, refers to underwater ocean currents:

[T]he fish of the sea that pass through the paths of the seas.

However, scientists did not know these paths or currents existed until the 1800s when Dr. Matthew Fontaine Maury discovered them. Today, ocean liners follow these currents, (which were popularized in the Disney film *Finding Nemo*). One of these, the Cromwell Current, travels more than 13,000 miles through the Pacific Ocean.

Earthquake Fault Line Through the Mount of Olives

The Jewish prophet Zechariah wrote in approximately 520 BCE that one day the Messiah will stand on the Mount of Olives in Jerusalem, and the mountain will split in two:

> His feet will stand on the Mount of Olives, which faces Jerusalem to the east. And the Mount of Olives shall be split in two...
>
> *Zechariah 14:4*

Today we know that Israel sits on the Syria-Africa Rift Valley, the largest fault line in the world.[50] The geological institute in Tel Aviv also uncovered a major earthquake fault line running through the Mount of Olives.[51]

Circumcision on the 8th Day

It is an ancient Jewish practice to circumcise male children on the 8th day. This instruction was set forth by Moses 3,900 years ago:

> He who is eight days old among you shall be circumcised...
>
> *Genesis 17:12*

Medical science has only recently discovered the incredible benefit of circumcising on precisely the 8th day. On that day a male's level of prothrombin and vitamin K, which promote blood clotting, reach their peak.[52] Clearly God knew of this phenomenon and thus instructed the Israelites to circumcise on the 8th day.

In addition, it has been found that circumcision protects against infections. In 1988 the California Medical Association endorsed circumcision as an "effective public health measure." (Resolution, March 1988).[53]

Additional Scientific Facts Noted in the Bible

Air Has Weight
The fact that air has weight was only established about 300 years ago; yet the Hebrew Scriptures mentioned this in the book of Job written approximately 2,500 years ago:

> From where then does wisdom come? And where is the place of understanding? It is hidden from the eyes of all living, and concealed from the birds of the air....God understands its way, and He knows its place. For He looks to the ends of the earth, and sees under the whole heavens, to establish a weight for the wind...
>
> *Job 28:20–25*

Blood Gives Life
In 1616, William Harvey discovered that blood circulation is critical for sustaining life—confirming what the Bible revealed 3,000 years earlier:

> For the life of the flesh is in the blood.
>
> *Leviticus 17:11*

Nuclear Bombs Will Exist One Day
Twenty-five hundred years ago the prophet Zechariah wrote of weaponry that would cause flesh to burn off of a body. Today we understand that nuclear and chemical weapons do precisely that:

> Their flesh shall dissolve while they stand on their feet.
>
> *Zechariah 14:12*

Water Evaporates
Today we understand that water evaporates and returns as rainfall. Solomon wrote this centuries ago in the Book of Ecclesiastes:

> All the rivers run into the sea, yet the sea is not full; to the place from which the rivers come, there they return again.
>
> *Ecclesiastes 1:7*

Circuit of the Wind

We now understand there is repetition in the processes of the universe, including the circuits involved in the way the wind blows. Solomon observed this phenomenon three millennia ago:

> The wind goes toward the south, and turns around to the north; the wind whirls about continually, and comes again on its circuit.
>
> *Ecclesiastes 1:6*

Germs Can Cause Disease

We now understand that germs can be transmitted and cause disease. Thousands of years ago in the Hebrew Scriptures we were instructed throughout *Leviticus 13, 14,* and *15* on the importance of washing and cleansing:

> …he shall…wash his garments and bathe his body in water…and so he will be clean.
>
> *Leviticus 14:9*

Mental Health Affects Physical Health

Today we understand that we can literally worry ourselves sick and that depression can translate into real physical problems. The Hebrew Scriptures revealed this to us 3,000 years ago:

> A sound heart is life to the body, but envy is rottenness to the bones.
>
> *Proverbs 14:30*

> A merry heart does good, like medicine, but a broken spirit dries the bones.
>
> *Proverbs 17:22*

Pork and Shellfish Transport Disease

In Leviticus, God instructed the Israelites not to eat pork and shellfish:

> [T]he swine…is unclean to you.
>
> *Leviticus 11:7*

> But all in the seas or in the rivers that do not have fins and scales…they are an abomination to you.
>
> *Leviticus 11:10*

In the 1860s we discovered that infected pigs can spread the disorder known as trichinosis[54] and shellfish carry viruses.[55] Additionally both of these forbidden animals are scavengers feeding on dead animals, an unhealthy practice.[56]

Perhaps this biblical foreknowledge played a role in many of the greatest scientists of all time vouching for the Bible's authenticity, including Sir Francis Bacon, Sir Isaac Newton, and Galileo Galilei:

> …a man cannot be too well studied in the book of God's word…[57]
>
> *Sir Francis Bacon*
> Formulator of the scientific method which stressed gathering data from experimentation and induction, and a founder of the Royal Society of London

> I find more sure marks of authenticity in the Bible than in any profane history whatsoever.[58]
>
> *Sir Isaac Newton*
> Formulated the theory of gravity and three laws of motion

> As to the [physical] propositions which are stated but not rigorously demonstrated, anything contrary to the Bible involved in them must be considered undoubtedly false and should be proved so by every possible means.[59]
>
> *Galileo Galilei*
> Physicist and astronomer who developed the concept of the mathematical laws governing the universe

Dr. Charles H. Mayo, a surgeon and the son of one of the co-founders of the renowned Mayo Clinic concurred:

> In sickness or in health, one can find comfort and constructive advice in the Bible.[60]

The Patriarchs in the Scriptures Really Lived

The lives of Noah, Abraham, Isaac, Jacob, Joseph, Moses, Elijah, Solomon, and David are discussed in detail in the Hebrew Scriptures. Countless historians not only acknowledge that these individuals lived but lived at the time and in the place recorded in the Hebrew Scriptures. In fact, there is more information corroborating the facts of their lives than the lives of some other historical figures, such as Christopher Columbus. We readily accept information we read about Columbus' life, as well we should. Why then is there such skepticism about the lives and teachings of the patriarchs recorded in the Hebrew Scriptures?

Many Renowned Americans Trust in the Bible

To trust in the authenticity of the Bible places you in the company of many renowned Americans:

- It is impossible to govern without God and the Bible.[61]
  George Washington

- The Bible is the best book in the world. It contains more than all the libraries I have seen.[62]
  John Adams

- The Bible makes the best people in the world.[63]
  Thomas Jefferson

- That Book, Sir, is the rock upon which our republic rests.[64]
  Andrew Jackson

- The Bible is the Anchor of our liberties.[65]
  Ulysses S. Grant

- No educated man can afford to be ignorant of the Bible.[66]
  Theodore Roosevelt

- The Bible is the best of all books, for it is the word of God and teaches us the way to be happy in this world and the next.[67]

  John Jay
  First Chief Justice of the U.S. Supreme Court

- Education is useless without the Bible....God's word, contained in the Bible, has furnished all necessary rules to direct our conduct.[68]

  Noah Webster

- The Bible is worth all the other books which have ever been printed.[69]

  Patrick Henry

- In the formative days of the Republic the directing influence the Bible exercised upon the fathers of the Nation is conspicuously evident....Our enemies are guided by...unholy contempt of the human race. We are inspired by a faith that goes back through all the years to the first chapter of the Book of Genesis: "God created man in His own image."[70]

  Franklin D. Roosevelt

A final quote is gruesome but poignant:

I prefer to believe those writers who get their throats cut for what they write.[71]

Blaise Pascal
French philosopher and mathematician
who developed the modern theory of probability

Skeptics Become Followers

Over the years, many brilliant authors, lawyers, and scholars have set out to disprove the Bible. In the process, something remarkable happened: the skeptics themselves became convinced that the Bible is true. Former skeptics include:

- C.S. Lewis, renowned author

- Josh McDowell, author or co-author of over 100 books

- Lee Strobel, author and host of the TV show *Faith Under Fire*

- General Lew Wallace, author of Ben Hur and Territorial Governor of New Mexico after the U.S. Civil War

- Dr. Frank Morrision, renowned attorney and author of *The Book that Refused to be Written*

- Sir William Ramsey, English scholar

Conclusion

I was the chief of skeptics but I have come to believe the authenticity of the Scriptures due to their supernatural knowledge. The writers of the Bible glorify God, not themselves in their writings. They point people to God, not themselves, as the wise one, the judge, and the redeemer, making the Book all the more credible to me. The timeless wisdom, historical and prophetic accuracy, and scientific foreknowledge reveal its divine inspiration. There is nothing quite like this in any other book. Perhaps Abraham Lincoln's words most accurately portray what I feel in my heart:

> I believe the Bible is the best gift God has ever given to man.[72]

Chapter 4

Argument
I am a good person and that's all that really matters

Many proclaim, "I am a good person and that's all that really matters." The problem with this line of reasoning is that when we pronounce ourselves "good," we tend to be extremely lenient on ourselves, approving the paths we have chosen. What I think is good behavior may not be what you think is good and vice versa.

> All the ways of a man are pure in his own eyes.
>
> *Proverbs 16:2*

I may think it is good to work late and leave my toddlers with my wife. My wife may disagree. I may think it is good to speed because it saves time. The Highway Patrol and my insurance company would disagree. I may think it is good to smoke a pack of cigarettes a day because it calms my nerves and curbs my appetite. My physician and loved ones may disagree. We can be quite proficient at rationalizing and justifying our own behavior. Our natural tendency is to elevate our thoughts and views to a God-like plane and to judge that we are good.

How do we know what is truly good? There *is* a standard. The Ten Commandments set forth some clear guidelines. Lying is wrong. Coveting is wrong. God establishes the standard in His Word. And, you know what? None of us, not even the patriarchs, score 100%. Abraham, Isaac, and Jacob all lied about matters so significant they were recorded in the Bible. Abraham did not trust God's promise of a son through his elderly wife Sarah, so he slept with his maid-servant Hagar. Joseph's brothers threw him in a pit, sold him into slavery, and then lied to their father about what had happened. Moses killed a man. King David committed adultery and lied about it.

Yet God did not revoke His covenant with these men. They repented and God used them mightily. The same can be true for you and me. God's desire is for us to turn to Him.

I used to feel that I did not sin…much. I now know that we all sin:

> For there is not a just man on earth who does good
> and does not sin.
>
> *Ecclesiastes 7:20*

> …there is no one who does not sin...
>
> *1 Kings 8:46 (NIV)*

The Hebrew prophet Isaiah called the people to repentance for their sins which separated them from God:

> But your iniquities have separated you from your
> God; and your sins have hidden His face from you,
> so that He will not hear.
>
> *Isaiah 59:1–2*

We each need to turn and receive the forgiveness God offers us. *Yom Kippur* (the Day of Atonement discussed in *Leviticus 23*) reminds us of this. On that day, Jewish people fast and pray for forgiveness of their sins (transgressions). Although we may think we are good—and may actually be good compared to others—we all require God's forgiveness. The Hebrew Scriptures speak of God's forgiveness for our sins:

> "Come now, and let us reason together," says the Lord, "Though your sins are like scarlet, they shall be as white as snow; though they are red like crimson, they shall be as wool."
>
> *Isaiah 1:18*

The Hebrew Scriptures also remind us that God looks at the heart, not our outward acts of righteousness that can be perfunctorily performed for self esteem and reputation:

> And all our righteousnesses are like filthy rags;
>
> *Isaiah 64:6*

I find it interesting that the Bible notes that Adam and Eve's sin was eating from the tree of the knowledge of good and evil. Why did God forbid them to eat from *this* tree filled with succulent fruit in the Garden of Eden? I believe it was because God did not want men and women to claim that *they* knew what was good and what was evil. That job is reserved for God and only God. He is the judge, not us.

Someone accused of a crime does not get to serve as the judge in the case. A defendant cannot even appear before a judge who is a friend or relative, but must face someone impartial who will determine whether the law was broken.

The same applies for our moral and spiritual lives. We will all face an impartial, supernatural judge who resides in heaven. He decides according to His rules. He is merciful, but the Scriptures repeatedly declare that we must first acknowledge our transgressions as the Jewish prophet Ezekiel admonished us to do around 500 BCE:

> Repent, and turn from all your transgressions, so that iniquity will not be your ruin.
>
> *Ezekiel 18:30*

None of us measures up to God's standard; we need His mercy and forgiveness to receive the gift of everlasting life that Daniel spoke of 2,600 years ago:

> And many of those who sleep in the dust of the earth
> shall awake, some to everlasting life, some to shame
> and everlasting contempt.
>
> *Daniel 12:2*

I recently learned at a weekend seminar that often we do not feel the power of God due to obstructions we place in His path. The instructor, Craig Hill, compared the power of God to the power provided by a car battery. The battery might be fully charged but the car will not start if the battery cables are corroded, obstructing the transmission of its power. We too can restrict the power of God from working in our lives. We clean our cables by repenting and turning to God.

I used to rationalize, "My good deeds far outweigh the bad." Imagine going in front of a traffic judge and pleading, "Your Honor, my good driving far outweighs my bad. I stop at *most* red lights." Do you think you would be found "not guilty?" The same is true with the ultimate judge who sits on the throne on high. We are all guilty in varying degrees and need His mercy and grace. But He is merciful and willing to pardon us if we will simply acknowledge our sins and our need for forgiveness.

Chapter 5

Argument

There are no absolutes.
Every person can decide what's best for him or her.

The Bible establishes standards and rules. But, believe it or not, these rules are actually incredibly liberating! They provide structure and order. Imagine a highway system without a center line. You could just drive wherever you wanted. What chaos! Envision this country without a constitution. We would have no legal foundation, no benchmark, no standards. This nation's founding fathers did not allow each citizen to simply choose what behavior he or she considered convenient or appropriate. Boundaries were set in place by the government in the form of laws. Similarly, our Creator established parameters for us.

We can choose to wander, enjoying the exhilaration of momentary freedom. Or we can stay within the plumb line established by God. I used to go through life creating my own rules. What a daunting challenge for anyone, especially a young person. I would create rules at one age and discard them a few years later. Would it have been wiser to simply trust in the rules given to us by the Creator of the universe?

We can look for solutions through our limited knowledge or put our confidence in the omniscience of God.

Truth is not determined by our subjective experiences and opinions, but rather by objective reality. If there were no absolutes and relativism were true, then the earth would contain numerous contradictory conditions and truths based upon our collective views. Certain conditions would exist for those who adopted them and would not exist for those who did not. Clearly this is not the case. The Bible establishes standards and rules that we can choose to either accept or reject—but denying their existence can cause adverse consequences just as denying the existence of gravity can result in a somber outcome.

God's Rules Are for Our Protection

Toddlers typically do not see the danger of wandering out into the street. However, when a youngster honors the instruction of his or her parents, the danger of being hit by a 4,000-pound automobile can be avoided. The same is true to an even greater degree when we follow the instructions of our heavenly father.

The Story of Nathan and the Freedom He Desired

The story of Nathan illustrates the beauty and blessing of boundaries and guidelines:

> *Once there was a young boy named Nathan who lived on a farm enclosed by a wooden fence. Nathan's father instructed him to never go beyond the fence alone as dangers lurked beyond it. Nathan honored his father's instruction for many years. One autumn day, as Nathan grew older and more independent, he decided to wander outside the fence. He saw beautiful fields and began to joyfully frolic through them chasing butterflies, turning over rocks, and thoroughly enjoying his freedom in these restricted areas.*

Nathan was totally enthralled and began to question why his father had confined him all those years. The fence seemed like an unnecessary and arbitrary restraint. Nathan grumbled to himself that the fence had been placed too close to his home. There was so much fun waiting on the other side.

After an afternoon of freedom and fun, enjoying the broader boundaries he had established, Nathan glanced up and realized that he had lost his bearings and had no idea where home was. Nightfall was setting in and it was becoming cold and dark. He was hungry and thirsty, but had no food or water. There was no shelter for warmth and protection, and he had not thought to bring a jacket. To make matters worse, he had cut his hand and was bleeding. He had no ointment or bandage to put on his gash.

Nathan began to long for his home and protection. He longed for his mother and father to comfort him and nurse his wound. But he did not know where they were or even how to find them. There were no markers in the wild showing him the way home. There he was without food and water and without a bandage, jacket, or blanket. He had no parents to turn to because he had ignored their rules and chosen his own. He was lost and scared. Oh, how he longed for a marker.

Just like Nathan, we are free to roam about enjoying a momentary thrill, ignoring boundaries and rules designed to protect us. But is that wise?

The Hebrew Scriptures Do Not Contain "Laws," They Contain "Instructions"

Did you know that the "laws" in the Hebrew Scriptures are not really laws? "Torah" is the word used in the Scriptures to describe the words given by God to Moses on Mount Sinai. "Torah" is frequently translated as "law," but it actually means "instruction." In other words, the Hebrew Scriptures contain our Creator's *instructions* for us, the ones He loves:

> I have loved you with an everlasting love.
>
> *Jeremiah 31:3*

I would actually be upset if the manufacturer of a product did not include instructions. Just recently, I could not figure out how to replace a bulb in my car. What did I do? I pulled out my owner's manual. I was so grateful for those instructions.

God presented us with a training manual to equip and guide us as we sojourn through life. We are free to either follow His instructions or ignore them. The choice is ours. Like King David the Psalmist, I have found the way of God to be far superior:

> As for God, His way is perfect; the word of the Lord
> is proven; He is a shield to all who trust in Him.
>
> *Psalm 18:30*

Chapter 6

Argument

God has not answered my prayers and seems distant

Many lose faith because God seems distant. Our prayers seem unanswered and our lives can be a struggle. However, we must remember that God is not a genie in a bottle promising, "your slightest wish is my command." If that were the case, we could simply request millions of dollars, perfect health, exquisite looks, and magnetic personalities.

Our Heavenly Father loves us with an everlasting love and knows what we need more than we do. His Word promises that *if* we delight ourselves in Him:

> He shall give you the desires of your heart.
>
> *Psalm 37:4*

God does not always perform according to our wishes. When our wills are not aligned with His, it may seem as if our requests are not being heard. Actually, the answer from God simply was not "Great idea! Why didn't I think of that?" Sometimes, a father in his wisdom must answer "no," "not now," or "wait." That is often God's answer as well. Parents typically do not supply everything their children request. If they did, there would be an abundance of junk food, a dearth of chores, an absence of curfews, an endless supply of video games, self-cleaning rooms with spectacular views, and unlimited cell phone minutes.

But why do our seemingly reasonable prayer requests go unanswered? That is a mystery that I have found unravels slowly as we grow in our faith and is revealed to each of us in God's perfect time. God knows what we need, just as parents know what is best for their beloved children. While we may pray that trials and hardships pass quickly, difficult times may be just what we need to learn patience and develop character. If God answered all my prayers I might love Him simply because He jumped when I said "jump."

Are there things I do not understand about God? Absolutely! But I trust God and have found that over time I have begun to understand matters I previously questioned. It seems that God desires to leave us with a few mysteries. Perhaps He planned it that way to humble us and encourage us to rely upon Him. King Solomon, considered by many to be the wisest man who ever lived, wrote:

> Trust in the Lord with all your heart, and lean not on your own understanding; in all your ways acknowledge Him, and He shall direct your paths.
> *Proverbs 3:5–6*

God does not perform as we think He should, because He is God. When we decide how life should be, we are, in essence, playing God. It would be similar to teenagers dictating to their parents when and if they will clean their room, come down for dinner, or return the car. Sounds kind of crazy, doesn't it? Parents would say, "Not so fast, I am still in charge." That is similar to God's response when we say, "If you really loved me, you would give me what I want." Would He? Would you?

I believe difficult times in our lives cause us to turn to God. I do not believe that God *causes* tragedies but He can work them for good.

Evil men—not God—caused the horrific events of September 11, 2001. However, we all remember how cohesive the United States became over the ensuing days. Republicans and Democrats gathered together on the steps of Congress and sang "God Bless America." That was virtually unprecedented unity! The 9/11 tragedy seemed to bring out the best in individuals. People risked their lives to save others and provided generous financial assistance to those in need. The same inspiring response followed Hurricane Katrina in September, 2005.

A lingering illness, painful as it can be, can be a time in which broken relationships are healed and we are reminded of what is truly important in life. Difficult times remind us that life is unpredictable and temporary, but a relationship with God is steadfast and everlasting.

Many of us have prayed for things years ago that we are now quite thankful did not happen. We may have prayed for a job we felt was ideal only to discover later that the company closed or treated its employees unfairly. We may have prayed that God send a certain mate our way only to visit with that person years later at a high school reunion and realize that God knew best after all. God answers prayers according to His divine plan, not human understanding. There is a Yiddish saying, "Man plans and God laughs." Our plans are not always His.

A recent event in my life underscores the blessing of unanswered prayer. In the spring of 2007 I began to experience discomfort in my lower back. It was so uncomfortable that I was forced to virtually eliminate my exercise routine. When my wife and I and two of our children traveled to Yosemite National Park, we were unable to hike on the long trails because I could only walk about 100 yards. I fervently prayed that God heal my back. No response; no healing.

One month later I was diagnosed with coronary artery disease. One of my main arteries was 95% blocked, and two of my collateral arteries were 100% blocked. All told, I had 13 blockages. Interestingly, our bodies sometimes create new collateral arteries as alternative routes for blood travel, and fortunately my body did that. Nonetheless, I needed open heart surgery for six coronary bypasses. Had I been able to hike in Yosemite as I desired, I may have died right there from a heart attack. I feel God was not answering the prayers to heal my back because He had a better plan—to save my life and strengthen my faith.

Several weeks after the surgery I was able to walk five miles without any discomfort in my back.

God knows exactly what we need for the long haul, and His Word promises that He will bless us:

> For the Lord your God will bless you just as He promised you.
>
> *Deuteronomy 15:6*

I have learned that I need to trust God in all circumstances. His wisdom far surpasses mine.

Chapter 7

Argument

If God spoke audibly or appeared to me I would believe in Him

God has revealed Himself through the intricate complexity of the world and the splendor of the Bible. Is more information really necessary? If he spoke audibly would I want Him to speak again so I could be *really* sure? He parted the Red Sea for the Israelites in order to save them from the pursuing Egyptians; a short while later they once again doubted Him. Arguments can be crafted that speak against the existence of God. However, to me, the magnificence, order, and balance of the universe and the intricately complex human body present irrefutable evidence of His existence. While additional reminders might be appreciated, are they really necessary? I concur with the conclusion noted previously of Ralph Waldo Emerson:

> All I have seen teaches me to trust the Creator for all I have not seen.[73]

A Trial Run with the Afterlife

It would be marvelous if we could *temporarily* die and then return to life. That little trial run with the afterlife would certainly help clarify issues pertaining to God—similar to receiving a taste sample at the supermarket.

If you tried dying and noticed a markedly increased temperature and encountered large numbers of unsavory characters with whom you would not want to be caught dead (sorry, I couldn't resist) and then returned to earth, your decision about how to live life would be simple. But God did not choose to do it that way. God chose not to let us witness the *after*life *before*hand and has left us with some mysteries.

If I were God, I would not have created a weed. However, I now realize the weed helps me appreciate lush green grass. If orchids abounded everywhere, they would be the norm and would no longer be special. If I were God I would not have created Canis Majoris, the huge star discussed in Chapter 2 that is 7 quadrillion times the size of the earth. I would have seen no value in it, especially being so far away. But God knew that we would marvel at such a massive formation, and it would creatively point us to His magnificence. Discovering the beauty of God is like holding a crystal at just the right angle so that it sparkles and displays the beautiful prism previously concealed from view.

God has a depth of understanding that far surpasses mine. I have learned to trust His game plan and listen with my heart.

Chapter 8

Argument
As long as you're happy, that's all that matters

We often hear people say, "As long as you're happy, that's all that matters," or "God just wants me to be happy." Let's stop and ponder the notion that God just wants you and your loved ones to be happy.

What if stealing, cheating, excessive drinking, or robbery makes you happy? Those involved with the terrorist attacks on the World Trade Center and Pentagon on 9/11 were just doing what made them happy—killing infidels. Can we really embrace an attitude that allows Nazis to do whatever makes them happy? The KKK? Gangs? Addicts? Can you imagine such a world?

Well, you might say, I just want to be happy as long as I do not hurt anyone else. Would it be OK if I watch TV all day? What if every day I eat six fast-food triple bacon cheeseburgers with extra sauce because it makes me happy? What if I decide not to study or go to class and pay someone to do my homework and write my papers? Or suppose I smoke three packs of cigarettes and drink two six packs of beer every day because it makes me happy? Those things might make some people quite happy and may not appear to harm others.

You may reply, "I won't do anything *that* extreme." Or, "Trust me, I will choose behavior that is reasonable—no one will be critical of my choices." The problem with that approach is we then have over 6.65 billion people on the planet each deciding what is reasonable behavior.

In an effort to create our personal happiness, we often tend to pick and choose the rules to follow and the standards *we* think should govern life. As discussed previously, it seems we need an external standard of what is acceptable behavior. Our society has many laws defining acceptable behavior. We are not permitted free reign to do as we please. God does not give us free reign either. He too, established parameters and put them in the Bible.

Fame and Fortune Is No Panacea

Many feel that the fame and fortune of a movie star would make them incredibly happy—and it might…for a while. In spite of acquiring fame and fortune, celebrities are often so discontented that they turn to drugs hoping for a quick fix and happiness. Britney Spears and Lindsay Lohan join a long list of celebrities who have had to check into alcohol and drug rehabilitation centers.[74] The tribulations of Paris Hilton are well documented. Robert Downey, Jr. has been in jail and rehab facilities. Wealth and public recognition are not the panacea many of us imagine they are. The divorce rate in Hollywood is extremely high. Money is no guarantee of lasting contentment and peace as the Scriptures noted millennia ago:

> The eyes of man are never satisfied.
>
> *Proverbs 27:20*

My Angst

I was a law student from a loving upper-middle class family. I had a promising career, had clerked at a prestigious law firm, and was interning in the prosecutor's office. I had a wonderful girlfriend, who is now my wife. Life was fantastic; I was quite happy. Many would have loved to change places with me. However, I was obsessed with myself—my interests, money, success, and career—and this created stress.

After passing the bar exam, I built a successful law practice, and my life seemed on the right path. I had other lawyers working for me and was earning a very nice living. Soon I moved to a larger and nicer office and home, thanks to two significant corporate clients that comprised 70% of my business. Within a few months, one of these clients sold the company and the other went out of business. My income dropped dramatically. I was filled with anxiety, my happiness disappeared, and I began to have difficulty sleeping. My dreams, plans, and ambitions were falling apart, and I had no control over them.

I was upset because things were not going as I thought they should, and this was impacting someone extremely important to me— Jim Jacob. I was focused on worldly success, which I had always assumed would make me happy. I discovered that goals can get derailed suddenly, and happiness can vanish instantly.

My rule had always been: "Work hard and take care of yourself." I did not need God or anyone else. Although I was happy for the moment, I did not have the kind of everlasting joy that could withstand the setbacks I now encountered. I faced those challenging years without the comfort and wisdom provided by God. Today when troubles arise I am much better equipped to endure them, knowing God is by my side.

Happiness Is Fleeting and Is Not the Same As Joy

The word "happy" comes from the same root as the word "happening"; it focuses on what is *happening* at the moment. We may even think we are happy right now. Life is good—decent job, nice home, committed spouse, lots of friends, and good health. But take any of that away, and many of us would become unhappy quicker than we can say "that's not fair!"

If what is "happening" vanishes, so too may the happiness. Seeking happiness can resemble grasping at the wind.

Joy, on the other hand, is contentment that remains despite what is happening. Happiness comes from the outside. Joy comes from within—an inner peace provided by the Creator of the universe who loves you and holds you in the palms of His hands:

> Surely they may forget, yet I [God] will not forget you.
> See, I have inscribed you on the palms of My hands.
> *Isaiah 49:15–16*

I have found that the only "filling" that lasts is the love of God. It seems that God made us that way—to long for Him. The automobile was designed so that gasoline makes it run. Caviar and fine wine will not make your car perform. In fact, they will cause great damage. The same is true with our "tanks." Only one thing fills it properly. Trusting in God is like saying, "I am going to fill up with high octane so I can function properly and be prepared for the challenges on the road of life."

Howard Hughes, at one point one of the wealthiest men in the world, seemed riddled with fear and eccentricities. Here is one account of how his life ended:

> He was a figure of gothic horror, ready for the grave. Emaciated, only 120 pounds stretched out over his six-foot-four-inch frame...thin scraggly beard that reached midway onto his sunken chest, hideously long nails in grotesque yellowed corkscrews.... Many of his teeth were black, rotting stumps. A tumor was beginning to emerge from the side of his head...innumerable needle marks....Howard Hughes was an addict. A billionaire junkie.[75]

Hollywood starlet Marilyn Monroe was considered one of the most beautiful women in the world in the 1960s. She had fame and fortune and was at the height of her career. She was married to Joe DiMaggio, perhaps the greatest baseball player in the world at the time. Yet, it is believed that Marilyn Monroe took her own life.

It has been reported that J. Paul Getty, at one time the world's wealthiest person, was a very discontented man. The same has been said of Jack Kent Cooke, the late owner of the Washington Redskins and a self-made billionaire. The idiosyncrasies and phobias of pop star Michael Jackson are widely reported.

One of the United States' leading researchers on happiness, Dr. Ed Diener, interviewed 49 of America's wealthiest people and found that 80% of them believe wealth can cause *un*happiness. Many factors play a role in this, from the demands assets place on your time to the stress associated with maintaining your lifestyle.[76]

Dr. Ronnie Janoff Bulaman and her colleagues compared 22 "average" people to major lottery winners; she found that over time the lottery winners reverted to their pre-lottery level of happiness (or depression) and ended up no happier than the average person.[77]

God's desire is that each of us turn our heart to Him and let Him fill us abundantly. Happiness, like most highs, is fleeting. It is nothing more than an illusion, a counterfeit of what true peace and joy can be. True peace and joy is from God, pierces our hearts, and is everlasting. God can fill you abundantly and happiness will seem shallow by comparison. As best-selling author John Ortberg stated, the condition of our heart is that "we need what nobody sells."[78]

What will bring you joy? A relationship with God has brought peace and joy to many, including me. It seems like it is worth a try.

Chapter 9

Argument

No one should impose a particular religious view on anyone else

Imposing or Sharing?

If I see someone smoking a cigarette while filling a car with gasoline, I would be very tempted to share with that individual the danger that is lurking. If I see someone driving without a seat belt, I might want to point out the risk he or she is taking.

Many like to share their latest discovery—from a bargain restaurant to a heartwarming movie to the latest fad diet. We want others to benefit as we have. If I had struggled to lose weight and was suddenly able to effortlessly shed pounds by following the rules in a diet book, I would certainly share that book with some friends.

Those Annoying Religious Folks

Those who wish to share beliefs about God and the afterlife are imperfect people like you and me. They probably aren't sharing the love of God with you because they get brownie points, a finder's fee, or 20% off their next purchase. They are probably sharing their genuine excitement about God with you because their lives have been miraculously, dramatically, and sometimes instantaneously changed. They probably care enough about you that they want your life to be changed too.

If Eating Pomegranates Could Save Your Life

Suppose you read in the newspaper about a study that surveyed hundreds of millions of people. The survey revealed that if you eat one pomegranate per day, you will generally feel better, your problems will not seem as overwhelming, and you will experience unimaginable tranquility. The survey also reported that after you die you will be transported to a paradise, in which there is no pain, war, taxes, commercials, deductibles, barking dogs, lies, fatigue, calories, telephone solicitors, housework, road rage, bills, inflation, pop quizzes, child labor, adult labor, traffic jams, or pollution. (I guess you now know all of my pet peeves!) You will live forever in this paradise—a land that is so wonderful that no mind can imagine how beautiful and special it is.

If you had read about these life-changing pomegranates, would you consider the claims about them? Would you do an Internet search on "pomegranates and heaven?" Would you ask friends their opinion of the study? Would you listen to someone on a street corner who offered further information on the study? Would you be willing to set aside your preconceived ideas about pomegranates and give them a shot?

Many who would seriously explore the mysteries of the pomegranate have no interest in exploring the mysteries of God. As I have already stated, I was a member of this non-seeker class for many years. Is it possible that something was stifling my curiosity? The Hebrew Scriptures promise that *if* we seek God with all of our heart, we *will* find Him:

Argument: No one should impose a particular religious view

> You will seek Me and find Me when you seek Me with
> all of your heart.
>
> *Jeremiah 29:13*

As we seek God, mysteries unravel and abundant blessings pour out.

Once you taste the sweetness of God, you will long for more of Him. I urge you to open your hearts to learn more about the love of God. You will not be disappointed!

Chapter 10

Argument
Religion is corrupt

Many reject God because they feel that organized religion is corrupt. It is true that there is often corruption, pride, and ambition associated with organized religion. However, is it *wise* to reject the message because you dislike the messenger?

If you feel that a certain place of worship or religious institution is corrupt, then by all means, have nothing to do with it. But please do not let the actions of disingenuous people cause you to reject the genuine message of love and forgiveness and the free gift of salvation that God offers.

If I was mugged while playing golf on a certain golf course, I may never play golf on that course again. However, I would not give up golf. I would find a new course.

A rope can be used to rescue someone or it can be twisted to create a hangman's noose or to tie up a hostage. The same rope that can save a life can also be misused. The same is true of Scripture. It can be twisted and misused, but that does not mean it is evil or dangerous in itself.

As previously noted, truth is not determined by our subjective experiences and opinions but rather by objective reality. We can shred an invoice that is sent to us and subjectively believe the debt is gone, but the reality is that the debt still exists. Similarly what we have subjectively experienced with religious organizations has no bearing on the reality of God.

Please do not give up on God because you had a bad experience at a synagogue or church. Rather, focus on God, and allow Him to become the source of your joy. Conversely, the leaders at a particular institution may be fine, upstanding individuals and even good role models, but they are not the ones in whom we should place our ultimate trust and faith.

Some dismiss the Bible because they feel that religion causes too much strife and division. It is true that proponents of certain religious beliefs use their faith to smugly set themselves above and apart from others. However, is that a reason to throw out the love of God? Certain eating disorders may result in illness or even death, but that is certainly not a reason to forego eating. Set your gaze upon God—not on His imperfect messengers. You won't be disappointed.

Chapter 11

Argument

If there is a God, why is there so much suffering?

Many feel that there cannot be a God because God would not have allowed the Holocaust and other atrocities. That is an interesting point which, at first blush, seems to make sense. But let's delve into that for a moment.

Clearly the Holocaust was caused by the choices of Adolf Hitler and the Nazis who supported him. Could God have stopped them? Yes. But had He intervened, He would have been interfering with free will. Would we want that? Probably—as long as God was putting a halt to the actions of our enemies. But what if God stopped *our* actions?

Imagine if God prevented us from pursuing our dream career because it was not His desire for our life? Or intercepted any money we earn above the most basic needs because He thinks we should donate the balance to the poor?

God loves us so much that He gives us free will to make our own decisions. Unfortunately, we do not always make wise choices. But how precious it is when we choose right over wrong and when we choose to love God.

Marriage in the free world is predicated upon people making their own choices as to whom they will marry. We cherish this freedom and would greatly resent being instructed as to whom we are to marry. In the same way, God has graciously granted us the free will to choose whether we will embark upon a relationship with Him.

History is overflowing with stories of oppressed people fighting for liberty—the right to be able to exercise their free will. People yearn for this freedom. Many have given their lives fighting for it, including Sir William Wallace who led a Scottish revolt against the oppression of England. Wallace's fight for freedom was dramatized in the 1995 Academy Award winning film, *Braveheart.*

There will always be people who exercise this free will in a manner that harms others. But during even the toughest times we can cling to the Word of God which promises:

> "For I know the plans I have for you," declares the Lord, "plans to prosper you and not to harm you, plans to give you hope and a future."
> *Jeremiah 29:11 (NIV)*

The state of Israel rose out of the ashes of the Holocaust. God gave the Jewish people a "hope and a future" by giving them a homeland shortly after the horrors of World War II.

The suffering that society endures from infirmities is often the result of free will as well. We suffer many illnesses and diseases because of bacteria and viruses that have developed due to the choices made by humankind over the centuries. For example, over the years we have introduced countless chemicals into our environment and food supply that have caused health problems. Additionally, a lack of proper hygiene and sanitation has created an incubator for the growth of bacteria which rapidly spreads due to increased global travel.

Illness and suffering befall us despite our best intentions. We can work out, eat healthy foods, and be in great shape, and then get hit by a car. We can build our dream homes, filled with priceless memorabilia, and they can all be destroyed by a flood or fire. We can build a great reputation and then be falsely accused of a crime. The only thing that can withstand life's trials and tribulations is our relationship with God. No one can take that from us, and it provides peace amidst the storms of life.

Corrie ten Boom was able to thank God for the lice in the concentration camps because they kept brutal Nazi guards away. As our faith and trust in God grows despite the circumstances, so too does our strength and peace:

> But those who wait on the Lord shall renew their strength; they shall mount up with wings like eagles, they shall run and not be weary, they shall walk and not faint.
>
> *Isaiah 40:31*

God works all things for good if we simply trust in Him during trials and cling to His promises. He does not make all of our troubles vanish, but He provides the strength to endure the trials that will ultimately refine and strengthen us.

Chapter 12

Argument

The Hebrew Scriptures do not speak of the Messiah coming 2,000 years ago

The Hebrew Scriptures Speak Extensively about the Messiah and Were 100% Accurate in Predictions Concerning the First Coming of the Messiah 2,000 Years Ago

The Hebrew Scriptures speak extensively about the Messiah who brings salvation to the world. In fact, there are over 300 predictions (prophecies) in the Hebrew Scriptures about the coming of the Messiah, and Yeshua (Jesus' Hebrew name) fulfilled *every* one of them. Imagine the odds!

In the late 1950s, Jeanne Dixon predicted the assassination of the next U.S. president. When the next president, John F. Kennedy, was assassinated in 1963, Ms. Dixon received a great deal of notoriety, even though she apparently had missed countless other predictions. Compare Ms. Dixon's success rate with that of the prophets in the Bible. The prophets in the Bible were correct literally 100% of the time!

Seven of the 300+ Messianic prophecies from the Hebrew Scriptures that Yeshua fulfilled approximately 2,000 years ago are:[79]

1. Prophecy:
The Messiah would be born in Bethlehem.
Bethlehem…out of you will come for me one who will be ruler over Israel, whose origins are from of old, from ancient times.

Micah 5:2 (NIV)

Fact:
Yeshua was born in Bethlehem.
See *Matthew 2:1–6, Luke 2:1–20.*

2. Prophecy:
The Messiah would enter Jerusalem on a donkey.
Shout, Daughter of Jerusalem! See, your king comes to you, righteous and having salvation, gentle and riding on a donkey…

Zechariah 9:9 (NIV)

Fact:
Yeshua entered Jerusalem riding on a donkey.
See *Matthew 21:1–9, John 12:12–16.*

3. Prophecy:
The Messiah would be rejected by His own nation.
He was despised and rejected by men…he was despised, and we [the Jewish people] esteemed him not.

Isaiah 53:3 (NIV)

The stone which the builders rejected has become the chief cornerstone.

Psalm 118:22

Fact:
Many of the Jewish people rejected Yeshua as the Messiah.
See *Matthew 26:3–4, John 12:37–43, Acts 4:10–12.*

4. Prophecy:
The Messiah would heal the blind, lame, deaf, and dumb.
Then the eyes of the blind shall be opened, and the ears of the deaf shall be unstopped. Then the lame shall leap like a deer, and the tongue of the dumb sing.
Isaiah 35:5–6

Fact:
Yeshua healed many, including the blind, lame, deaf, and dumb.
See *Matthew 11:4–6, 15:30–31.*

5. Prophecy:
The Messiah would die for the sins of the world.
We all, like sheep, have gone astray, each of us has turned to his own way; and the Lord has laid on him the iniquity of us all...he was led like a lamb to the slaughter... for the transgression of my people he was stricken.
Isaiah 53:6–8 (NIV)

Fact:
Yeshua took the punishment for us all and died for the sins of the world.
I encourage you to read all of *Isaiah 53* which is in Appendix B. Please decide for yourself whether *Isaiah 53* describes Yeshua. The Talmud, a central text in Rabbinic Judaism, acknowledges that *Isaiah 53* does refer to the Messiah. See *Sanhedrin 98a.*

See *John 1:29, John 19, 1 Timothy 1:15,* and other passages throughout the Messianic writings (New Covenant).

6. Prophecy:
The Messiah would be crucified.
...they have pierced my hands and my feet...people

stare and gloat over me. They divide my garments among them and cast lots for my clothing.

Psalm 22:16–18 (NIV)

But he was pierced for our transgressions, he was crushed for our iniquities; the punishment that brought us peace was upon him, and by his wounds we are healed.

Isaiah 53:5 (NIV)

Just as there were many who were appalled at him— his appearance was so disfigured beyond that of any man and his form marred beyond human likeness…

Isaiah 52:14 (NIV)

Fact:
Yeshua was crucified.
See *Matthew 27:35, Luke 24:33–34, 39–40.*

Interestingly, *Psalm 22* referenced above was written in approximately 1,000 BCE and *Isaiah 52* and *53* referenced above were written in approximately 700 BCE; yet crucifixion does not appear to have even been invented until 600 BCE or later!

7. Prophecy:
The Messiah would be resurrected.
…because you will not abandon me to the grave, nor will you let your Holy One see decay.

Psalm 16:10 (NIV)

Fact:
Yeshua rose from the dead three days after his death.
See *Acts 2:23–36, 13:33–37, Matthew 28:1–20.*

In addition, the ancient Jewish prophet Daniel established when the Messiah would die. *Daniel 9* clearly states that the Messiah would be "cut off" (die) at a certain time, namely 69 (62 +7) "weeks" of years or 69 x 7 years (483 years) after the order to rebuild Jerusalem (which occurred in *approximately* 444 BCE. See *Nehemiah 2:1*). So *Daniel 9* predicts the death of the Messiah in *approximately* 39 CE. Moreover, if the 483 years are converted from the lunar calendar (360 day year) used at the time of Daniel to the solar calendar (365 day year), the year Daniel prophesied for the Messiah's death becomes 32 CE, the approximate year many historians place Yeshua's historic resurrection! (483 years x 360 days=173,880 days ÷ 365.25 [.25 to account for leap years] = 476 years. 476 years after 444 BCE is 32 CE). Thus, the Messiah had to come at the time of Yeshua!

In this passage Daniel also wrote that after Yeshua's death, animal sacrifice offerings would no longer be necessary for the forgiveness of sins. The reason animal sacrifices would no longer be necessary is that Yeshua was the full and final atoning sacrifice.

Daniel 9 prophecies:

> ...from the issuing of a decree to restore and rebuild Jerusalem until Messiah the Prince {there will be} seven weeks and sixty-two weeks....Then after the sixty-two weeks the Messiah will be cut off and have nothing, and the people of the prince who is to come will destroy the city and the sanctuary....And he will make a firm covenant with the many...he will put a stop to sacrifice and grain offering;
>
> *Daniel 9:25–27 (NAS)*

Some of the early rabbis also confirm in the Talmud that the Messiah would come during the time of the Second Temple.[80] The Second Temple period was from 515 BCE to 70 CE.

See www.hopeoftheworld.com for the Rabbinic Mysteries teaching series which discusses other writings of the ancient Rabbis which point to Yeshua as the Messiah (tapes 731, 745, 804, and 860).

Additionally, prophecies Yeshua fulfilled can readily be found in many books and on the Internet. Recall that Chapter 3 contains prophecies in the Hebrew Scriptures pertaining to Israel that have also been fulfilled with 100% accuracy.

Passages in the Hebrew Scriptures
Clearly and Boldly Refer to God's Son

The Hebrew Scriptures boldly proclaim that God will have a son and that His son is also God. Below are six of the passages that address these matters.

1. *Proverbs 30:4* **unequivocally acknowledges that God, the Creator, has a son.**
> Who has gone up to heaven and come down? Who has gathered up the wind in the hollow of his hands? Who has wrapped up the waters in his cloak? *Who has established all the ends of the earth?* What is his name, and the name of *his son? (NIV)*

2. *Psalm 2:7* **clearly refers to the Lord speaking to His Son.**
> I will proclaim the decree of the Lord: He said to me, *"You are my Son;* today I have become your Father." *(NIV)*

3. *Isaiah 9:6* **unequivocally mentions a son who is also "Mighty God."**
> For unto us a *child is born,* to us a *son is given,* and the government will be on his shoulders. And *he will be called* Wonderful Counselor, *Mighty God,* Everlasting Father, Prince of Peace. *(NIV)*

4. *Genesis 1:26* **records God referring to the Creator as "us."**
> Let *us* make man in *our* image. *(NIV)*

The word "us" is plural so it has to be referring to God and *someone else,* both of whom have supernatural capabilities as together they create man. This passage clearly states that someone else assisted with the creation and that man was made in the image of God *and* this assistant. Who could this supernatural assistant be other than God in the form of a man?

5. *Isaiah 6:8* **again refers to God in the plural.**

> Then I heard the voice of the Lord saying, "Whom
> shall I send? And who will go for *us?*" *(NIV)*

6. *Zechariah 12:10* **refers to the One whom the people have pierced,
who is like a firstborn son.** Yeshua was pierced (crucified) and hung
on a cross and was the firstborn son of God.

> And I will pour out on the house of David and on the
> inhabitants of Jerusalem a spirit of grace and suppli-
> cation. They will look on me, the one they have
> *pierced,* and they will mourn for him as one mourns
> for an *only child,* and grieve bitterly for him as one
> grieves for a *firstborn son. (NIV)*

Passages in the Hebrew Scriptures
Clearly Refer to God Taking the Form of a Man

Many feel that God could not become a man. Yet the Hebrew
Scriptures repeatedly document God appearing as a man. Read these
passages and decide for yourself. How comforting to recognize that
God so loved us that He became a man so He could fellowship with us,
minister to us, and die to atone for our transgressions.

1. *Genesis 3:8* **describes God walking in the Garden of Eden.** If God
was walking, it seems He was a man.

> And they heard the sound of the Lord God *walking* in
> the garden in the cool of the day...

2. *Genesis 18:1–3* **clearly mentions that the Lord appeared but
Abraham only saw three men, one of whom is God, and Abraham
addresses as "My Lord."**

> Then *the Lord appeared to him* by the terebinth trees
> of Mamre, as he was sitting in the tent door in the
> heat of the day. So he lifted his eyes and looked, and
> behold, *three men* were standing by him; and when
> he saw them, he ran from the tent door to meet them,

and bowed himself to the ground, and said, "*My Lord,*
if I have now found favor in Your sight, do not pass
on by Your servant."

3. In *Genesis 32:24–30,* Jacob wrestles with a man and then says he has now seen God, face to face.

So Jacob was left alone, and a *man* wrestled with him
till daybreak....The *man* asked him, "What is your
name?" "Jacob," he answered. Then the *man* said,
"Your name will no longer be Jacob, but Israel,
because y*ou have struggled with God* and with men
and have overcome." So Jacob called the place Peniel,
saying: "It is because *I saw God face to face,* and yet
my life was spared." *(NIV)*

4. In *Exodus 24:9–10,* God has feet...just like a man.

Moses and Aaron, Nadab and Abihu, and the seventy
elders of Israel went up and *saw the God of Israel.*
Under his feet was something like a pavement made of
sapphire, clear as the sky itself. *(NIV)*

5. *Exodus 31:18* describes God writing the 10 Commandments with His finger.

...He gave Moses two tablets of the Testimony, tablets
of stone, written with the *finger of God.*

6. *Psalm 110:1* records that God spoke to God and asked Him to sit, so God must be speaking to another being who is also God and can sit.

The *Lord says to my Lord,* "Sit at my right hand, until
I make your enemies a footstool for your feet." *(NIV)*

7. *Zechariah 9:9* foretells that the Messiah will come bringing salvation and riding on a donkey. Only a human can ride a donkey and this man is extraordinary as He also brings salvation.

See, your *king* comes to you, righteous and having
salvation, gentle and *riding on a donkey... (NIV)*

8. *Isaiah 48:16* **records God being present from the beginning of time and God referring to Himself, His Spirit, and a third person whom He sent.** Here God is discussing His triune nature. This will be discussed further in Chapter 13. The three forms of God are used interchangeably in this passage. The pronoun "me" in the first sentence is God (as no one else could have spoken from the beginning of time—the time of the "first announcement") and the "me" in the second sentence is someone sent by God. The second sentence refers to three forms of God: "Lord," "me" (who is the speaker and has already been identified as being God), and "his Spirit." I have added the brackets to help illuminate these references.

> Come near to *me* [God] and listen to this: From the
> first announcement I [God] have not spoken in secret;
> at the time it happens, I [God] am there. And now
> the Sovereign Lord [God] has sent *me,* [a third person,
> Yeshua] with his Spirit [Spirit of God]. *(NIV)*

9. *Daniel 7:9* **refers to multiple thrones in heaven for God.** Why would there be a need for more than one throne unless God took on two forms?

> I watched till *thrones* were put in place...

10. *Psalm 45:7* **again refers to God in two forms—God and God's God.**

> ...therefore God, *your God,* has set you above your
> companions by anointing you with the oil of joy. *(NIV)*

11. *Zechariah 2:10–11* **refers to the Lord stating that the Lord has sent me to dwell in our midst just as the Messianic writings say Yeshua was sent to dwell in our midst.**

> "...For I am coming and I will live among you,"
> declares the Lord...and you will know that the *Lord*
> *Almighty has sent me to you.* (NIV)

12. *Ezekiel 1:26–28* **refers to a man above the sky on a God-like sapphire throne with "brilliant light" surrounding him. This man is described as having the "likeness of the glory of the Lord."**

> Above the expanse over their heads was what looked
> like a throne of sapphire, and high above on the

throne was a figure like that of a *man*. I saw, that from what appeared to be his waist up *he* looked like glowing metal, as if full of fire, and that from there down *he* looked like fire; and brilliant light surrounded *him*. Like the appearance of a rainbow in the clouds on a rainy day, so was the radiance around *him*. This was the appearance of the *likeness of the glory of the Lord*. When I saw it, I fell facedown, and I heard the voice of one speaking. *(NIV)*

13. In *Joshua 5:13–15*, Joshua bows before a man and refers to Him as "Lord."

Now when Joshua was near Jericho, he looked up and saw a man standing in front of him with a drawn sword in his hand....Then Joshua fell face down to the ground in reverence, and asked him, "What message does my Lord have for his servant?" The commander of the Lord's army replied, "Take off your sandals, for the place where you are standing is holy." And Joshua did so. *(NIV)*

Verses Describing the Time of Messiah Yeshua's Return

The Scriptures state that the Messiah will not return until:

1. Control of Jerusalem is returned to the Jewish people, and
2. The Jewish people recognize Yeshua as the Messiah.

Two passages quoted below clearly elucidate this—*Luke 21* and *Matthew 23*. The first event occurred in June, 1967 when Israel regained control of Jerusalem during the Six Day War. The second criterion for the return of Messiah—Jews coming to faith in Yeshua—is coming true today...at a rapid pace. Author and Pastor Don Finto believes it is possible that 500,000 Jewish people have come to faith in Yeshua since 1967.

Luke, a nice Jewish doctor,[81] writes that Jerusalem will be "trampled by the Gentiles [nations]" for many years and then it will be returned to the Jews (this occurred in 1967). This same passage foretells that the generation that sees the Jews regain control of Jerusalem will also see the return of Messiah:

> ...*Jerusalem will be trampled by Gentiles until the times of the Gentiles are fulfilled.* And there will be signs in the sun, in the moon, and in the stars; and on the earth distress of nations, with perplexity, the sea and the waves roaring; men's hearts failing them from fear and the expectation of those things which are coming on the earth, for the powers of heaven will be shaken. *Then they will see the Son of Man* [a term often used to describe the Messiah] coming in a cloud with power and great glory. *Now when these things begin to happen, look up and lift up your heads, because your redemption draws near.*...So you also, when you see these things happening, know that the *kingdom of God is near.* Assuredly, I say to you, *this generation will by no means pass away till all things take place.*
>
> *Luke 21:24–32*

We do not know how many years a "generation" is in God's eyes, so we do not know the day or the hour of His return. However, we can recognize events that indicate we are in the "season" of His return. Among the reasons we know this season has begun is that Yeshua announced that He would not return until the Jewish people recognize Him as the Messiah:

> ...you [the Jewish people] shall see Me no more till you [the Jewish people] say, "Blessed is He [Yeshua] who comes in the name of the Lord!"
>
> *Matthew 23:39*

So when the Jewish people recognize Yeshua as the Messiah, we know we are close to the time of His return!

Today both criteria have been met. Jerusalem is in Jewish control for the first time in nearly 2,000 years, and the Jewish people are accepting Yeshua as their Messiah in far greater numbers than ever before. What is even more amazing is that the beginning of this outpouring of belief in Yeshua among Jewish people miraculously coincided with the return of Jerusalem to Jewish control in 1967. At that time there were only a handful of Jewish believers in Yeshua and there were barely any Messianic congregations. Messianic congregations consist of Jews and Gentiles that worship Yeshua in a Jewish fashion, recognizing and celebrating the festivals established in the Hebrew Scriptures. These holy days include *Pesach* (Passover), *Shavuot* (Feast of Weeks or Pentecost), *Rosh Hashanah* (New Year), *Yom Kippur* (Day of Atonement), *Sukkot* (Feast of Tabernacles), and *Shabbat* (Sabbath). At the beginning of 2008, there were over 150 Messianic congregations in Israel alone and about 650 worldwide.[82] In June 2008 *Time* magazine estimated that there may be as many as 15,000 Messianic Jews living in Israel.[83]

While most branches of Judaism are experiencing a decline, Messianic Judaism is growing and flourishing—despite opposition! The opposition seems to be declining as people are recognizing that Messianic Jews are not *mishugah* (crazy). In 2007 Israeli television aired an objective and somewhat favorable story about Messianic Judaism.[84]

I have found that Messianic Jews love God, Israel, and Jewish people in a powerful way, and love to worship God. At the congregation my family and I attend, about 80–90% of the members show up every week for Shabbat services! I actually look forward to Shabbat services! It is not something I dread and *kvetch* (complain) about.

Visitors to the congregation I attend often indicate that they experience a love and warmth there they have never felt anywhere. They also comment that the music is very uplifting. Jews are not only finding their Messiah, they are worshiping Him in an exciting and personally meaningful way.

It seems clear that the significant growth of Messianic Judaism is a prophetic move of God and a sign that the Messiah's return to Israel is near. The Jewish people are undergoing a change of heart and accepting the Messiah they had previously rejected, precisely as Ezekiel prophesied 2,500 years ago:

> I will...bring you into your own land. I will sprinkle clean water on you....*I will give you a new heart [for*

Yeshua] and put a new spirit [Spirit of God] in you; I
will remove from you your heart of stone and give
you a heart of flesh. And *I will put my Spirit in you*
and move you to follow my decrees and be careful to
keep my laws.

Ezekiel 36:24–27 (NIV)

Conclusion

Yeshua came the first time as a Suffering Servant who was crucified.
He died for the sins of the world, and His death brought salvation
(forgiveness and eternal life) to the world for those who trust in Him.
His Word promises He will return as an everlasting King! Hallelujah!

...all peoples, nations and languages should serve
Him. His dominion is an everlasting dominion which
shall not pass away, and His kingdom the one which
shall not be destroyed.

Daniel 7:14

God is faithful! His promises come true! We are seeing His
promises unfold in the days in which we live. He is returning soon!

Chapter 13

Argument
There is no evidence that God had a son who was also God

Would the Disciples Lay Down their Lives and Die for an Impostor?

It is universally accepted that Yeshua walked the earth approximately 2,000 years ago (see *The World Book Encyclopedia*), and that He hand-picked 12 disciples, asking them to give up everything they had and follow Him—which they did! You may have heard of some of them: Matthew, John, Judas (the Betrayer), Peter, and (Doubting) Thomas. Would these disciples give up everything they owned if Yeshua was an impostor—just an ordinary man? Perhaps. Some have followed impostors, but usually these impostors spread strange teachings and offer no witnesses to their miracles. This was not the case with Yeshua. *His miracles were witnessed by thousands of people* and His teachings were far from eccentric—they illuminated the timeless wisdom of the Torah such as "love your neighbor as yourself" and the Golden Rule—"Do unto others as you would have others do unto you" *(Leviticus 19:18, Matthew 7:12, Matthew 22:39)*.

What motivated the disciples, and countless others, to sacrifice *everything* for this man? Why were they willing to be tortured, imprisoned, and stoned to death for following Him? Because they watched—with their own eyes—Yeshua walk on water and heal the sick. They observed Him exhibit love and forgiveness toward those who spoke against Him and those who whipped, scourged (lashed with a jagged edged metal whip), and finally crucified Him. Through all of this torment, He neither fought back nor complained. Events pertaining to His life and ministry are documented in secular reference books as well as the Bible.[85]

I know of no human who could exercise such restraint and compassion—do you? When I get falsely accused, I tend to become a little defensive. It is human nature to defend oneself, especially when wrongfully accused. Yeshua was falsely accused of not being the Son of God. Did He throw around His weight, defend Himself, and curse His accusers? Not at all! He prayed for and blessed His accusers and cried out, "Father, forgive them, for they do not know what they do" *(Luke 23:34)*. He did this after He had been brutally punished, nailed to a cross, and was near death. Would an imposter be in a merciful state of mind and pray for those who had done these cruel things to him? Only a special person could possibly demonstrate such grace.

Like a lamb at Passover, Yeshua was led to slaughter. A slaughter He did not deserve. He was laid in a grave by those He came to save, yet He did not complain. That is the type of God I wish to serve. He laid down His life, so that you and I could have everlasting life. *Hallelujah! Baruch HaShem!* (Bless His Name!)

Yeshua Claimed to be the Son of God and God Manifest in the Flesh

Yeshua claimed to be the Son of God *(Luke 22:70)* whose coming the Jewish prophets had predicted. At the Festival of Lights *(Hanukkah)* in Jerusalem, Yeshua also proclaimed that He was God when he proclaimed, "I and My Father are one" *(John 10:30)*.

I think we can agree that claiming to be God is extremely bold. As author C.S. Lewis eloquently pointed out in the book *Mere Christianity,* a person making the claim that he is God is either a liar, lunatic, or Lord (i.e., he is who he claims to be). Only a liar or lunatic would make such a claim if it were not true.

There is no evidence whatsoever of Yeshua being either a liar or lunatic. None, zip, nada. He interacted intelligently with Jewish scholars and leaders. No one ever found fault with His character except those who felt He lied when He claimed to be God. Yeshua would not have been motivated to proclaim this for very long if it were not true, as it immediately had the religious authorities wanting to torture and kill Him.

Most Jewish scholars today acknowledge that Yeshua was a stunningly brilliant rabbi and that His teachings were insightful, rich, and timeless. If He is neither a liar nor lunatic, and He claimed to be God in the flesh, then He must be who He said He was.

Let's scrutinize other teachings of Yeshua to see if they seem either deceptive or deluded. All of His teachings seem to clearly be from a righteous man. Here are several:

> Blessed are those who hunger and thirst for righteousness, for they shall be filled.
>
> *Matthew 5:6*

> Blessed are the merciful for they shall obtain mercy.
>
> *Matthew 5:7*

> Blessed are the pure in heart, for they shall see God.
>
> *Matthew 5:8*

> Blessed are the peacemakers, for they shall be called sons of God.
>
> *Matthew 5:9*

> Let your light so shine before men, that they may see
> your good works and glorify your Father in heaven.
>
> *Matthew 5:16*

> You shall love the Lord your God with all your heart,
> with all your soul, and with all your mind.
>
> *Matthew 22:37*

Are these the teachings of a lunatic?

Additional Passages in the Hebrew Scriptures that Refer to God in the Plural

When asked what was the most important commandment, Yeshua responded that it was the *Shema*. The *Shema* is perhaps the most well-known prayer in Judaism. This famous prayer from *Deuteronomy 6:4* refers to God in the plural in two places:

> *Shema Yisrael, Adonai eloheynu, Adonai echad.*
> Hear, oh Israel, the Lord our God, the Lord is one.

First, this passage uses the Hebrew word *eloheynu* which literally means "our Gods." Judaism makes it clear that there is only one God so this cannot be referring to more than one God. Perhaps it is referring to three forms of God united as "one"—God the Father in heaven, the Son of God on earth (Yeshua), and the Spirit of God?

This passage also includes the word *echad* at the end to describe the oneness of God. The use of the word *echad* also denotes that this prayer is referring to different forms of God united as "one." *Echad* is translated as "one" but literally means "complex unity," i.e., the Lord is a "complex unity." Scripture also refers to a husband and wife becoming *echad* when they wed. That is, they are still two people but they are also united together as one. In this prayer the same is being said about the Lord—He is a complex unity, united as one. *Yachid* could have been chosen for the word "one" but was not. *Yachid* means "singular" or "only."

We have already considered that at the time of creation God refers to Himself in the plural. "Let *us* make man in *our* image" *(Genesis 1:26, NIV)*. Also, in the well-known words of the opening of Genesis, Moses writes—"In the beginning, God created the heavens and earth." The Hebrew word used for "God" in this passage is "*Elohim*," the plural form of God.

Isaiah 6:8 (NIV), again refers to God in the plural when God asks:

> Whom shall I send? And who will go for *us?*

Further, as noted in the preceding chapter, the Hebrew Scriptures indeed discuss the triune nature of God (Father, Son, and Spirit of God) in *Isaiah 48:16*. Interestingly, after Yeshua's ascension to heaven, the third form of God, the *Ruakh HaKodesh* (the Spirit of God or the Holy Spirit), was sent on *Shavuot* (Feast of Weeks or Pentecost) to dwell within us. *Shavuot* commemorates the day God gave Moses the *Law* of God on Mount Sinai written on tablets of stone. On this exact same day over a thousand years later, the *Spirit* of God was given to us and is written on our hearts *(Acts 2:1–4)*.

The *Ruakh HaKodesh* helps me to love God with my mind and spirit. It is analogous to the fuel for a jet airplane:

> But you shall receive power when the Holy Spirit has come upon you.
>
> *Acts 1:8*

The *Ruakh HaKodesh* is my comforter and guide. It nurtures my spirit in ways previously unimaginable, and helps me understand what God can accomplish in me when I surrender my heart to Him.

At the Beginning of the Hebrew Scriptures Is the Gospel Message of Yeshua Bringing Rest and Comfort

God has many interesting messages in His Word. One that I find particularly intriguing is that He has placed the gospel message at the beginning of the Hebrew Scriptures! Gospel simply means "good news" and is a term that refers to the first four books of the Messianic writings that record the life of Yeshua written by Matthew, Mark, Luke, and John. The gospel message is that sin separates us from God, but Yeshua, God in the flesh, came to earth to die for our sins and restore us to Himself. His atoning death brings us comfort and allows us to be made righteous before a holy God.

God embedded this message in the names given to Adam and his lineal descendants down to Noah. The Hebrew names of these descendants, in order, are Adam, Seth, Enosh, Kenan, Mahalalel, Yared, Enoch, Methuselah, Lamech, and Noah. Noah is nine generations removed from Adam. If Adam and his lineal descendants are lined up one right after the other, the gospel message is revealed to us when their names are translated from Hebrew to English. For example, *Adam* is Hebrew for *man*. *Seth* is Hebrew for *appointed*. Below is a listing of the names of Adam and his descendants in chronological order with their translation:

Adam	=	Man
Seth	=	Appointed
Enosh	=	Mortal
Kenan	=	Sorrow
Mahalalel	=	The blessed God
Yared	=	Shall come down
Enoch	=	Teaching
Methusaleh	=	His death shall bring
Lamech	=	The despairing
Noah	=	Comfort

When you put this together you have a sentence that reads, "Man appointed mortal sorrow the blessed God shall come down teaching; His death shall bring the despairing comfort." So at the very beginning of the Torah, God plants the message of salvation—the blessed God shall come down and teach, and by His death, those in despair shall be comforted because His atoning sacrifice cleanses us of our sins and removes our separation from God.[86]

If we look for Him, we will find Him in the Torah as well as in the rest of the Hebrew Scriptures, the universe, and our lives.

Evidence and Logic Point to an Empty Tomb

After being scourged and crucified by professional Roman executioners, a spear was struck into Yeshua's side and blood and water emptied out *(John 19:34)*. This provided post-mortem evidence of His death which today doctors understand was probably caused by heart failure due to shock and constriction of the heart brought on by excess fluid in the pericardium (the sac enclosing the heart).[87] The crucifixion was performed before countless witnesses who would certainly announce to the world if they believed that Yeshua was not dead. It seems abundantly clear, to even the highly skeptical mind, that He was really dead.

Yeshua was then laid in a grave that was sealed with a huge stone that took several men to move. Surely the Romans guarded the tomb with the utmost care and caution, given the hot political climate surrounding this man. They certainly did not want Yeshua's body to be tampered with or removed. The Romans feared that if Yeshua was believed to be God then His followers might swear allegiance to Him, not Rome. So they undoubtedly assigned their most reliable guards to this tomb. They did not have Deputy Barney Fife of Mayberry on duty.[88] These guards understood that they would be killed if anyone was allowed to steal the body of this high-profile prisoner.

Yeshua's enemies had no motive to remove His body and His followers had no access to the tomb. Yet, three days later, the tomb was empty! If the tomb was not empty, the already-decaying body would have been produced and this charade would have ended long ago.

So what happened? Magic? Poor reporting by the Gospel writers? This was an extremely important event in Israel at the time. It seems the writers had to get it right, or many skeptics would investigate and report the truth. Yeshua's resurrection was an event that shook all of Israel. If it did not actually occur, surely those who opposed Yeshua would have preserved contradictory evidence. Yet there is not one shred of contradictory evidence.[89]

No rebuttal witness was produced—not one. The body was never found. He was seen alive by over 500 witnesses *(I Corinthians 15:5–8)*. The only plausible conclusion is that Yeshua was resurrected from the tomb just as was written centuries ago by King David:

...nor will you let your Holy One see decay.

Psalm 16:10 (NIV)

Notable Scholars, Logicians, and Historians Dissect the Evidence and Become Followers of Yeshua

The book *The Resurrection Factor* by Josh McDowell provides six powerful testimonies of renowned scholarly individuals who thoroughly scrutinized the evidence of Yeshua's resurrection and concluded it was irrefutable! Among the testimonies are those of the following individuals:

1. **Dr. Simon Greenleaf** (1783–1853) was born Jewish and became one of the founders of Harvard Law School. He wrote a famous three-volume reference book for trial lawyers entitled *A Treatise on the Law of Evidence*. After extensively dissecting the evidence for the resurrection, Greenleaf became a follower of Yeshua. He became thoroughly convinced that there is more evidence for the resurrection of Yeshua than for virtually *any* other event in history. Greenleaf later authored a scholarly book on the evidence of the resurrection entitled *Testimony of the Evangelists Examined by the Rules of Evidence Administered in the Court of Justice*. In it, he stated that he "confidently believed" that the four gospels are not forgeries and the oldest copies would be admitted into evidence in a court of law as genuine and truthful documents.[90]

2. **Dr. Paul L. Maier**, graduated from Harvard in 1954 and is a professor of ancient history at Western Michigan University. He concluded that, "If all the evidence is weighed carefully and fairly, it is indeed justifiable, according to the canons of historical research, to conclude that the tomb in which Jesus was buried was actually empty....And no shred of evidence has yet been discovered in literary sources, epigraphy, or archaeology that would disprove this statement."[91]

3. **Lord Charles Darling** (1849–1936), a former Chief Justice in England affirmed "...no intelligent jury in the world could fail to bring in a verdict that the resurrection story is true."[92]

4. **John Singleton Copley** (1738–1815), three times the High Chancellor of England and elected High Steward of the University of Cambridge, is recognized as one of the greatest attorneys in British history. He declared that "evidence…for the resurrection has never broken down yet."[93]

World-Renowned Scientists and Legendary Individuals Also Become Followers

Here is a short list of great thinkers and statesmen who were followers of Yeshua:[94]

1. **Michelangelo Buonarroti.** One of the greatest artists in history.

2. **Sir Walter Raleigh.** Navigator, writer, courtier, and colonizer.

3. **Sir Francis Bacon.** Philosopher, essayist, courtier, jurist, and statesman.

4. **Galileo Galilei.** Mathematician, physicist, and astronomer credited with conceiving of the idea for the isochronous pendulum and sector-compass; he developed the concept of mathematical laws governing the universe.

5. **Sir Isaac Newton.** Mathematician and natural philosopher who discovered the laws of universal gravitation, formulated the three laws of motion, which aided in advancing the discipline of dynamics, and helped develop calculus into a comprehensive branch of mathematics.

6. **Louis Pasteur.** Microbiologist and chemist, Pasteur developed the process of pasteurization for milk, the vaccines for anthrax and chicken cholera (1881), and the rabies vaccine (1885). He revolutionized the medical field by establishing the germ theory of disease, organic basis and regulation of fermentation, and bacteriology.

7. **Johannes Kepler.** One of the founders of modern astronomy, Kepler discovered the laws governing planetary motion, and pioneered the discipline of celestial mechanics, known as Kepler's Laws, which aided Newton in his formulation of the theory of gravitation.

8. **Werner Van Braun.** Father of the U.S. space program.

9. **Ludwig van Beethoven.** One of the greatest composers in human history.

10. **George Frideric Handel.** One of the foremost composers of the Baroque era.

11. **Johann Sebastian Bach.** One of the foremost composers of the Baroque era.

12. **Wolfgang Amadeus Mozart.** Composer and piano virtuoso; renowned musical genius.

13. **John Harvard.** First benefactor of Harvard College, now Harvard University.

14. **John Locke.** Philosopher, diplomat, and educator, whose writings profoundly influenced America's Founding Fathers.

15. **William Penn.** Founder of Pennsylvania.

16. **Samuel Adams.** Revolutionary leader and signer of the Declaration of Independence.

17. **George Washington.** First President of the United States.

18. **John Adams.** Second President of the United States.

19. **Abraham Lincoln.** Sixteenth President of the United States.

20. **Patrick Henry.** American Revolutionary leader and orator, remembered for proclaiming, "Give me liberty or give me death!"

21. **John Hancock.** An American Revolutionary leader, graduate of Harvard, and the first to sign the Declaration of Independence.

22. **General Douglas MacArthur.** Recipient of Medal of Honor and prominent U.S. general in World War II.

23. **Martin Luther King, Jr.** Prominent civil rights leader.

24. **Sir Francis Scott Key.** American lawyer who penned "The Star Spangled Banner."

25. **Samuel Morse.** Inventor of the Morse Code, he developed the telegraph and built the first U.S. camera.

26. **Jedediah Morse.** Pioneer American educator and geographer; he was dubbed the "Father of American Geography."

27. **Hans Christian Anderson.** Novelist and story-writer. He authored many fairy tales, including *The Ugly Duckling*, *The Emperor's New Clothes*, and *The Tinder Box*.

28. **William Shakespeare.** English playwright whose works have had an enduring worldwide impact.

29. **Henry Wadsworth Longfellow.** Renowned American poet.

30. **Charles Dickens.** Legendary British author.

31. **Leo Nikolaevich Tolstoi.** Russian playwright and novelist, most famous for writing *War and Peace*.

32. **Booker T. Washington.** American educator, writer, and reformer. Born a slave, he was the first African American to have his picture on a U.S. postage stamp and his image on a U.S. coin.

33. **George Washington Carver.** Discovered numerous medical uses for the peanut.

34. **J.C. Penney.** Businessman, entrepreneur, and founder of the J.C. Penney chain of retail stores.

Please also consider the following proclamations by prominent individuals who recognize the lasting significance and veracity of the Bible:

> Education is useless without the Bible.[95]
>
> *Noah Webster*
> Compiler of *Webster's Dictionary*

> The Bible is the cornerstone of liberty. A student's perusal of the sacred volume will make him a better citizen, a better father, a better husband.[96]
>
> *Thomas Jefferson*

> The existence of the Bible, as a book for the people, is the greatest benefit which the human race has ever experienced. Every attempt to belittle it is a crime against humanity.[97]
>
> *Immanuel Kant*
> Philosopher

> Men blaspheme what they don't know.[98]
>
> *Blaise Pascal*
> Father of the Science of Hydrostatics,
> who helped develop the barometer

I leave you with the following observation by Christopher Columbus (who some historians believe was Jewish) from his travel diary. He speaks of God giving him the notion to sail to the New World and the inspiration he received from the Holy Spirit:

> It was the Lord who put into my mind (I could feel His Hand upon me) to sail from here to the Indies....There

is no question that my inspiration was from the Holy Spirit....No one should fear to undertake any task in the name of our Savior, if it is just and if the intention is purely for His Holy service....O what a gracious Lord, Who desires that people should perform for Him those things for which He holds Himself responsible! Day and night, moment by moment, everyone should express to Him their most devoted gratitude.[99]

The Creator of the Universe Can Do Supernatural Things

The same God who created life can surely resurrect a life, especially when it is that of His Son sent to redeem the world. Some say they cannot believe that a resurrection of the dead can occur. Most of us struggle with supernatural things. To me, the creation of the universe is far more miraculous than someone being healed or raised from the dead.

Perhaps God is speaking to your heart right now. He wants to bring you into a righteous relationship with Him. But He won't force you. Does any of this resonate with you? If so, then ask God right now to assure you that He is real, loves you, and wants to forgive you for your past. Ask Him to come into your life and He will.

Chapter 14

Argument

I do not like organized religion

The decision is not whether organized "religion" is right for you or whether a certain religious group is right for you. Religions are created by people. The issue has nothing to do with religion or religious practices and customs. The issue is whether you wish to follow God.

God wants a relationship with you. This refreshing thought is certainly not something I heard when I was growing up. I had no idea that God wanted to be intimately involved in my daily life.

Is God real? Chapter 2 presented evidence that He is indeed real. Does He desire for you to follow Him and have a relationship with Him? *Psalm 73:28* proclaims that He desires for us to draw near to Him:

> But it is good for me to draw near to God.

If we draw near to Him we can have a relationship with Him. He instructs us to pray—to communicate with Him. Communicating helps build relationships. Some may hear an audible voice from God. I never have. I believe that most who have a relationship with God will tell you that God communicates with them through a still, small voice they sense in their inner being. He then provides confirmation that they have heard from Him. For example, if they feel God tells them to make peace with a person, that person may suddenly cross their path. If they feel He has led them to a certain Scripture verse, someone may call them and mention the identical verse.

Frequently God puts someone on my wife's heart. When He does this, she typically starts praying for them; she may even call them. Invariably she learns that they were going through a challenging time at that very moment. The Lord may even lead my wife to a Scripture that she shares with them that powerfully speaks into their circumstances. God is faithful! His Word confirms this:

> Therefore know that the Lord your God, He is God, the faithful God who keeps covenant and mercy for a thousand generations with those who love Him and keep His commandments.
>
> *Deuteronomy 7:9*

Job 33:26 explains that our prayers actually cause God to delight in us and to restore us to Him:

> He shall pray to God, and He will delight in him, he shall see His face with joy, for He restores to man His righteousness.

What a beautiful picture!

Relationship, not religion, is God's desire for His children. Religion is simply a framework within which people choose to worship an awesome God. Human beings have created many different types and branches of religion, and more seem to surface every day. True, there are some corrupt people involved in ministry. But I urge you—do not let these misguided people prevent you from worshiping your Creator and being fascinated by Him.

While considering this, please keep in mind that in the Hebrew Scriptures, God promises:

> ...whoever calls on the name of the Lord shall be saved [delivered].
>
> *Joel 2:32*

When I sought Him and called upon His name, I found Him. I believe the same can happen for you. His Word makes that very promise.

The most important decision you will ever make is whether you will accept Yeshua as your Messiah. If God exists and has a Son who came and died for you, then clearly having a relationship with God would be awesome. As Creator of the universe, God can radically transform your life, wipe away tears of bitterness and despair, lift you up on eagle's wings to heights you never imagined, and give you peace amidst the storms of life. A new life is awaiting you.

Chapter 15

Argument

It's not Jewish to believe in Jesus

Jesus was a Jew. In fact, His real name was Yeshua which is Hebrew for "salvation." His Jewish mother would shout, "Yeshua, come to dinner." (Of course, He would come without having to be called a second time!) Yeshua lived a Jewish life. He did not attend a church—there were no churches 2,000 years ago! At that time, the only people who believed in the Bible were the Jews, and they gathereed in synagogues.

Yeshua went to synagogue *(Luke 4:16)*. He placed *tzitziot* (fringes) on the four corners of his garments *(Matthew 14:36)*. He was born and lived in Israel. He was circumcised on the eighth day *(Luke 2:21)*. He referred to Himself as the "King of the Jews"*(John 19:21)*. His mother's name was actually Miryam.

Yeshua's followers called him "Rabbi." His coming to Israel, to bring salvation to the world, had long been foretold in the Hebrew Scriptures written by Hebrew prophets with Jewish names such as Isaiah, Daniel, Ezekiel, Jeremiah, and Zechariah. Zechariah prophesied, as recorded in the Hebrew Scriptures, that in the last days, the Messiah would stand on the Mount of Olives in Israel and *everyone* on earth would celebrate *Sukkot* (Feast of Tabernacles) in Jerusalem:

> His feet will stand on the Mount of Olives...[and] all the nations which came against Jerusalem shall go up from year to year to worship the King, Lord of hosts, and to keep the Feast of Tabernacles.
> *Zechariah 14:4, 16*

Yeshua celebrated the Sabbath from sunset on Friday to sunset on Saturday and recited Jewish blessings over wine and bread. It is interesting that Yeshua condoned the ceremonial drinking of wine, and today it is reported that one glass of red wine per day is healthy and may reduce heart disease.[100]

Yeshua studied and taught from a Torah scroll. He was 100% Jewish and loved the Jewish people. He celebrated the biblical festivals as instructed in the Hebrew Scriptures. As previously noted, these festivals include *Pesach* (Passover), *Shavuot* (Feast of Weeks or Pentecost), *Rosh HaShanah* (Feast of Trumpets), *Yom Kippur* (Day of Atonement), *Sukkot* (Feast of Tabernacles), and *Shabbat* (Sabbath).

Each one of Yeshua's disciples was Jewish. Every word in the Messianic writings was recorded by Jewish followers of Yeshua, known today as Messianic Jews.[101] Paul wrote a good deal of the Messianic writings and is often referred to as "St. Paul," but his name was Rabbi Saul of Tarsus.

The original followers of Yeshua were all Jewish. In fact, in those early days, there was an issue as to whether Gentiles could be followers of Yeshua.[102] Today, the issue has turned 180 degrees. Now the question is, "can a Jew believe in Yeshua and still be Jewish?" The answer is a resounding "yes!" Jews who believe in Yeshua are "completed" Jews who believe in the complete Bible. Messianic Jews believe what Rabbi Saul of Tarsus recorded in *Romans 11* that in the end "all Israel will be saved" and that the acceptance of Yeshua by Jewish people will be "life from the dead." It does not get much better than that now, does it?

For if their being cast away is the reconciling of the world, what will their acceptance be but *life from the dead?*...And so *all Israel will be saved,* as it is written: "The Deliverer [Messiah] will come out of Zion [Israel], and He will turn away ungodliness from Jacob [Jews]; for this is My covenant with them [Jews], when I take away their sins."

Romans 11:15, 26–27

Albert Einstein, a Jew, Nobel Prize winner, and professor at Princeton University, acknowledged his intrigue concerning Yeshua:

As a child I received instruction both in the Bible and in the Talmud. I am a Jew, but I am enthralled by the luminous figure of the Nazarene.[103]

Consider, too, these comments by other scholarly Jews who acknowledge the Jewishness of Yeshua and His lifestyle:

Jesus was a Jew and a Jew he remained till his last breath. His one idea was to implant within the nation the idea of the coming of the Messiah and, by repentance and good works, hasten the "end...." In all this, Jesus is the most Jewish of Jews...more Jewish than Hillel. From the standpoint of general humanity, he is, indeed, "a light to the Gentiles."[104]

Joseph Klausner
Author and former professor at
Hebrew University, Jerusalem

Jesus was utterly true to the Torah, as I myself hope to be. I even suspect that Jesus was even more true to the Torah than I, an Orthodox Jew....I accept the resurrection not as an invention of the community of disciples, but as an historical event.[105]

Dr. Pinchas Lapide
Jewish Orthodox scholar

It is a peculiar manifestation of our exile-psychology that we permitted, even aided in, the deletion of New Testament Messianism, that meaningful offshoot of our spiritual history. It was in a Jewish land, that this spiritual revolution was rekindled; and Jews were those who had spread it all over the land....We must overcome the superstitious fear which we harbor about the Messianic movement of Jesus, and place the movement where it belongs, namely, in the spiritual history of Judaism.[106]

Martin Buber
Author and former professor at
Hebrew University, Jerusalem

Everything He ever said or did has value for us today, and that is something you can say of no other man, alive or dead....He became the Light of the world. Why shouldn't I, a Jew, be proud of it?[107]

Sholem Asch
Yiddish novelist and author

Jesus was not only a Jew but he was the Jew, the Jew of Jews....In that day when history shall be written in the light of truth, the people of Israel will be known not as Christ-killers, but as Christ-bearers; not as God-slayers, but as the God-bringers to the world.[108]

Rabbi Stephen S. Wise
Zionist leader and founder of the
Jewish Institute of Religion

Below is one final quote from Benjamin Disraeli, Jewish Prime Minister of Great Britain in 1868, who came to know his Messiah:

Christians may continue to persecute Jews and Jews may persist in disbelieving Christians, but who can deny that Jesus of Nazareth, the incarnate Son of the Most High God, is the eternal glory of the Jewish race?[109]

Argument: It's not Jewish to believe in Jesus

For a listing of prominent Jews who believed in Yeshua see http://www.messianicassociation.org/profiles.htm. This website notes that there are over 200,000 Jewish believers in Yeshua in the United States alone. The list includes:

- Felix Mendelssohn, composer

- Rabbi Isaac Lichtenstein, Chief Rabbi of Hungary[110]

- Rabbi Leopold Cohn, Rabbi in Hungary

- Rabbi Israel Zolli, Chief Rabbi of Rome

- Rabbi Daniel Zion, Chief Rabbi of Bulgaria during the Holocaust[111]

- Niels Bohr, Nobel Prize for Physics

- Henry Bergson, Nobel Prize for Literature

- John Xeres, Talmudic Scholar

- Daniel Landsmann, Talmudic Scholar

- Boris Kornfeld, medical doctor, hero of the Gulag who led Alexander Solzhenitsyn to faith in the Messiah

- Andrew Mark Barron, Aerospace Engineer

- Mortimer Adler, Professor at the University of Chicago

- Jay Sekulow, attorney and founder of the American Center for Law and Justice

- Lawrence Kudlow, U.S. Undersecretary of the Office of Management and Budget

Time magazine has recognized that a paradigm shift is occurring in "rediscovering Jesus the Jew" in His Jewish context. On March 12, 2008, *Time* magazine noted that one of the great upcoming revolutions will be the re-Judaizing of Jesus.[112]

Additionally, the concept of a resurrection from the dead has Hebraic roots and can be found throughout Jewish literature. I kid you not! The *Shemoneh Esreh* or *Amidah* (Eighteen Benedictions or Standing Prayer), the central prayer in the Jewish *siddur* (prayer book) refers to God resurrecting the dead when it states:

> Blessed art Thou, O Lord, who *revives the dead.*

Additionally a resurrection from the dead is recorded in the Hebrew Scriptures:

> When Elisha came into the house, there was the *child, lying dead* on his bed. He went in therefore, shut the door behind the two of them, and prayed to the Lord. And he went up and lay on the child, and put his mouth on his mouth, his eyes on his eyes, and his hands on his hands; and he stretched himself out on the child, and the flesh of the child became warm...; then the child sneezed seven times, and *the child opened his eyes.*
>
> *2 Kings 4:32–35*

When Jews become followers of Yeshua they are not "converting to Christianity." They are doing something very Jewish—finding the Messiah of Israel who died for the salvation of Jews and Gentiles.

Lastly, consider the significant comments of Rabbi Isaac Lichtenstein (1824–1909). Rabbi Lichtenstein was the Chief Rabbi of Hungary. He led congregations for 40 years before he read the Messianic writings for the first time. After reading the Messianic writings he became a passionate follower of Yeshua. He noted how mistaken he had been and acknowledged:

> I had thought the New Testament to be impure, a source of pride, of hatred, and of the worst kind of violence, but as I opened it, I felt myself peculiarly and wonderfully taken possession of by a sudden glory, a light flashed through my soul. I looked for

thorns, and gathered roses, I discovered pearls instead of pebbles; instead of hatred, love; instead of vengeance, forgiveness; instead of bondage, freedom; instead of pride, humility; instead of enmity, conciliation; instead of death, life, salvation, resurrection, heavenly treasure.[113]

Chapter 16

Argument
I don't need to be saved from anything

The Hebrew Scriptures Declare that
Blood Atones for Our Sins

Leviticus 17:11 clearly states that "blood makes atonement" for our sins:

> For the life of the flesh is in the blood, and I have
> given it to you upon the altar to make atonement for
> your souls; for it is the blood that makes atonement
> for the soul.

Isaiah 59:1–2, Ezekiel 18:30 and *Daniel 12:2*, which are all discussed in Chapter 4, illustrate that our sins separate us from God and that we must atone for our transgressions to be reconciled with God and have everlasting life (saved). Before the destruction of the Second Temple in

70 CE, the blood of a goat atoned for the sins of the people. On *Yom Kippur*, the Day of Atonement, the High Priest went into the Holy of Holies within the Temple, and sprinkled the blood of a goat upon the mercy seat and altar to atone for the sins of the world *(Leviticus 16)*. Since the Temple is gone, how do we atone for our sins today?

Just as God provided Abraham the ram caught in a thicket as a substitute for the sacrifice of his only son Isaac *(Genesis 22)*, God has provided His Son Yeshua as a substitute sacrifice for us. The shedding of Yeshua's blood is the full and final sacrifice that takes away the sins of the world just as Yochanan the Immerser (John the "Baptist"—who was actually a Jew) proclaimed:

> The next day, Yochanan saw Yeshua coming toward him and said, "Look! God's lamb! The one who is taking away the sin of the world!"
>
> *John 1:20 (CJB)*

Yeshua's sacrifice was the fulfillment of the "new covenant" which was spoken of by the Jewish prophet Jeremiah in the Hebrew Scriptures 2,600 years ago:

> Behold, the days are coming, says the Lord, when I will make a *new covenant with the House of Israel* and with the house of Judah....I will put My law in their minds, and write it on their hearts; and I will be their God, and they shall be My people. No more shall every man teach his neighbor, and every man his brother, saying, "Know the Lord," for they all shall know Me, from the least of them to the greatest of them, says the Lord. For *I will forgive their iniquity, and their sin I will remember no more.*
>
> *Jeremiah 31:31–34*

There is a God. We are accountable to Him. He provided a plan for our salvation: to repent of our sins and accept the sacrifice of His Son as forgiveness for our transgressions. His blood covers our sins and makes atonement for them. Hallelujah!

Argument: I don't need to be saved from anything

In the Hebrew Scriptures, King David acknowledged that we are all in need of salvation which allows us to escape from death. In other words, we can have eternal life through God who saves us:

> Our God is a God who saves; from the Sovereign Lord comes escape from death.
>
> *Psalm 68:20 (NIV)*

Won't you join me right now? Your salvation is just a prayer away. Confess your sins before Him, ask His forgiveness, and invite Yeshua into your heart.

Chapter 17

Argument

The Bible is outdated and has nothing to do with my life in the 21st century

Did you know that many meaningful expressions we use in our every day 21st century life actually come from the Bible? In fact, you have probably preached the Bible yourself and not even known it.

Here are some examples of common expressions you may use that originated in the Bible:

1. Kiss of death *(Luke 12:47–48)*

2. Go the extra mile *(Matthew 5:4)*

3. By the skin of my teeth *(Job 19:20)*

4. There is nothing new under the sun *(Ecclesiastes 1:9)*

5. Turn the other cheek *(Matthew 5:39)*

6. The forbidden fruit *(Genesis 2:16–17)*

7. Patience of Job *(Job 2:3)*

8. Blinded by the light *(Acts 1:1–9)*

9. Blind leading the blind *(Matthew 15:14)*

10. Road to Damascus experience *(Acts 1:1–9)*

11. Eye for an eye and tooth for a tooth *(Exodus 21:22)*

12. Fuel for the fire *(Ezekiel 21:32)*

13. Spare the rod and spoil the child *(Proverbs 13:24)*

14. Scapegoat *(Leviticus 16:10)*

15. Do unto others as you would have others do unto you *(Leviticus 19:18, Matthew 7:12)*

16. He who desires to be first shall be last *(Mark 9:35)*

17. The truth shall set you free *(John 8:32)*

18. Prodigal son *(Luke 15:11–32)*

19. Land of milk and honey *(Exodus 3:8)*

20. Doubting Thomas *(John 20:19–31)*

21. Right hand man *(Mark 16:19)*

22. Cross to bear *(Mark 15:21)*

23. A three-strand cord is not easily broken *(Ecclesiastes 4:12)*

24. An olive branch *(Genesis 8:11)*

25. Love of money is the root of all evil *(1 Timothy 6:10)*

26. Thorn in my side *(2 Corinthians 12:7)*

27. Idle hands are the devil's workshop *(Job 10:3)*

28. O you of little faith *(Matthew 6:30)*

29. Feet of clay *(Genesis 2:7)*

30. Salt of the earth *(Matthew 5:13)*

31. Spring cleaning—from the Passover removal of leaven out of the home *(Exodus 12:15)*

32. Am I my brother's keeper? *(Genesis 4:9)*

33. Apple of His eye *(Zechariah 2:8, Psalm 17:8)*

34. Eat, drink, and be merry *(Ecclesiastes 8:15)*

35. Better to give than to receive *(Acts 20:35)*

36. Man does not live by bread alone *(Matthew 4:3–4)*

37. Don't cast pearls before swine *(Matthew 7:6)*

38. Walk on water *(Matthew 14:22–32)*

39. A house divided against itself will not stand *(Matthew 12:25)*

40. Iron sharpens iron *(Proverbs 27:17)*

Clearly, the words in the Bible written hundreds of years ago contain timeless wisdom that is relevant to our lives today.

Chapter 18

Argument

It is a waste of time to read the Bible

Do you feel it is you against the world? Do you frequently experience frustration dealing with life? Are you searching for peace? Then I urge you to read the Bible, an instruction manual lovingly prepared for your benefit. To help you remember what the Bible is, think of the word "Bible" as an acronym for Basic Instructions Before Leaving Earth—the instruction manual our Manufacturer provided as a guide for life.

The Bible is a book that millions of people have read over and over throughout their lives. *Time* magazine recognizes the Bible as the most influential book ever! *Time* further notes that "not only is the Bible the best-selling book of all time, it is the best-selling book of the year every year."[114] The Bible is a unique and miraculous book. Perhaps you have read portions and not found this to be the case. May I suggest that you try reading it again, but before you start, ask God to open your heart to receive His timeless wisdom.

I have found that the Bible provides soothing comfort to my mind, body, soul, and spirit. Since it is God's living Word it breathes life into my very being:

> In the beginning was the Word, and the Word was with God, and the Word was God. He was in the beginning with God. All things were made through Him, and without Him nothing was made that was made. In Him was life, and the life was the light of men.
>
> *John 1:1–4*

However, when I was growing up and heard a Bible story, I typically found it dry and boring. That was partially due to the fact that I did not have someone to assist me. Just as would-be carpenters apprentice with experienced carpenters, many people need someone to guide them as they begin to read the Bible. If you have trouble understanding the timeless instructions in the Bible, I suggest you find a good Bible study or a friend who can help you. To find a good Bible study, I would recommend that you contact either: a) a local Messianic Congregation which can be found in the Yellow Pages under Synagogues or see the International Alliance of Messianic Congregations and Synagogues (866-IAMCS-NOW or www.iamsc.org), b) Bible Study Fellowship, a non-denominational international Bible study that is in most large U.S. cities—I attended this for several years—see www.bsfinternational.org, or c) a church that recognizes the significance of Israel today and the Jewish roots of the faith.

There are a few who can build a car by simply reading an instruction manual. Most of us would have an easier, less frustrating time with an experienced automotive expert guiding us. Perhaps your circle of friends does not include someone with knowledge of the Bible and you cannot find a good Bible study. Why not pray for God to send someone to help you and for God to direct your path? God will provide!

Chapter 19

My Story
How my life was miraculously changed

My Life in the Jewish Community

I was born in 1953 and raised in a Jewish home in predominantly Jewish neighborhoods in the suburbs of St. Louis, Missouri. Virtually all of my grade-school classmates were Jewish. I worked at a Jewish summer camp and frequented the Jewish Community Center. I never really knew any Christians intimately—occasionally I saw people dressed up on Sunday morning going to church together as a family, looking clean and angelic. What a wholesome, all-American, apple pie, Wally and the Beaver sight—and how totally foreign and distant it all seemed to me.

In my secluded life, growing up within the Jewish community, I certainly did not discuss spiritual issues. Even though I went to Hebrew school and religious school, I knew very little about the Hebrew Scriptures. I was like many Jews—a cultural, secular Jew who simply identified with my heritage.

I was proud of my Jewish heritage and the contributions my people made to society, from Hollywood to Wall Street. Consider the contributions and accomplishments of the following people, all who are Jewish:

> Albert Einstein, Jonas Salk, Irving Berlin, Aaron Copeland, Leonard Bernstein, George Gershwin, Johann Strauss, Bob Dylan, Steven Spielberg, Oliver Stone, Sam Goldwyn and Louis B. Mayer (of Metro-Goldwyn-Mayer), Jerry Seinfeld, Adam Sandler, Robin Williams, Groucho Marx, each of the Three Stooges, George Burns, Kirk Douglas, Paul Newman, Michael Landon, Mike Wallace, Barbara Walters, Harry Houdini, David Copperfield, Herman Wouk, Marc Chagall, Calvin Klein, Ralph Lauren, Levi Strauss, Marc Spitz, Hank Greenberg, Sandy Koufax, Bobby Fischer, Red Auerbach, U.S. Supreme Court Justices Felix Frankfurter, Louis Brandeis, Benjamin Cordozo, and Abe Fortas, Alan Greenspan, Henry Kissinger, Joseph Pulitzer, Ann Landers, and Abigail (Dear Abby) Van Buren.

Growing up, I did not yet understand that these accomplishments were a fulfillment of God's promise to the Jewish people in *Genesis 12:1–3*:

> Now the Lord had said to Abram: "Get out of your country, from your family and from your father's house, to a land that I will show you. *I will make you a great nation;* I will bless you and make your name great; and you shall be a blessing. I will bless those who bless you, and I will curse him who curses you; and *in you all the families of the earth shall be blessed.*"

I now know that this *Genesis 12* promise has also been fulfilled by God using the Jewish people to give the world the Bible, the prophets, and the Messiah Himself.

My Story: How my life was miraculously changed

God has kept His promise that all the families of the earth will be blessed by Israel. Consider these contributions by Israel in its 60 years of existence, all while engaged in regular wars with relentless enemies who seek its destruction and with an economy continuously under strain by having to spend more per capita on its own protection than any other country on earth:

1. Israelis developed the cell phone at the Motorola lab in Haifa.

2. TransChip, an Israeli company, developed the first high-resolution camera for use in cell phones.

3. Most of the Windows NT and XP operating systems were developed at Microsoft-Israel.

4. The Pentium MMX Chip technology was designed in Israel at Intel.

5. Checkpoint, an Israeli company, pioneered Internet and network security technology such as Firewall.

6. The first PC anti-virus software was developed in Israel in 1979.

7. Voice mail technology was developed by NICE Systems, Amdocs, and Comverse, all Israeli companies.

8. Technology for the AOL Instant Messenger ICQ was developed in 1996 by four young Israelis.

9. TEVA, the world's largest maker of antibiotics and a world leader in generic drugs, is an Israeli company. TEVA fills one in every 15 prescriptions in the U.S. and has developed Azilect (rasagiline), an FDA approved drug which helps reduce shaking in patients suffering from Parkinson's disease.

10. Israeli scientists developed the first fully computerized, non-radiation, diagnostic instrumentation for breast cancer.

11. Given-Imaging, an Israeli company, developed the first ingestible video camera, so small that it fits inside a pill and can be swallowed. The camera helps diagnose digestive tract diseases.

129

12. Researchers in Israel developed a device that helps the heart pump blood, an innovation with the potential to save lives among those with heart failure. The new device is synchronized with a camera and helps doctors diagnose the heart's mechanical operations through a sophisticated system of sensors.

13. Israel leads the world in the number of scientists and technicians in the workforce per capita, with 145 per 10,000. (There are 85/10,000 in the U. S., over 70/10,000 in Japan, and less than 60/10,000 in Germany.)

14. Israel has the highest ratio in the world of university degrees to total population.

15. A new acne treatment developed in Israel, the Clear Light device, produces a high-intensity, ultraviolet-light-free, narrow-band blue light that causes acne bacteria to self-destruct—all without damaging surrounding skin or tissue.

16. Solel, an Israeli company, was the first to develop and install a large-scale solar-powered, fully functional electricity generating plant in southern California's Mojave desert.

17. M-Systems, an Israeli company, developed Disk on Key, the first and most powerful portable key chain storage on the market, the sales of which broke records, selling 250,000 units per month in 2007.

18. Israel has the second largest number of companies traded on Wall Street.

19. Hadassah Hospital in Jerusalem is home to a world-renowned burn center that has been used to treat Iraqi children burned in the Iraq war.

20. Israelis established a temporary eye clinic for Sudanese Refugees in Kenya.

21. A delegation of Israeli volunteers, masking their Jewish identity, visited a refugee camp in Somalia. They risked their lives to save Muslim refugees.

22. In 2008, Israel's Zetiq Technologies developed CellDetect, a simpler, more accurate cancer detection test that dramatically increases the sensitivity of cancer diagnosis.

23. More than 85% of solid waste in Israel is treated in an environmentally sound manner.

24. Israel is home to the largest concentration of high-tech industries in the world, relative to its population.

Growing up, I did not know the history of my people. I knew nothing about God's miraculous protection of the Jewish people over thousands of years or God's plans for the Jewish people, whom the Hebrew Scriptures call the apple of God's eye:

> ...for he who touches you [Israel] touches the apple of His eye.
>
> *Zechariah 2:8*

I did not know that on the first day Israel existed as a nation in 1948, five Arab nations defied the United Nations and simultaneously attacked Israel from all sides. Israel did not even have an army at the time, yet Israel won this war! Israel winning that war is comparable to New Jersey, without an army, prevailing against an attack by a country the size of the United States. This stunning victory was undoubtedly the greatest military upset of all time. The only logical explanation for this victory is that God was protecting His people's return to their land, just as He said He would:

> For I will take you from among the nations, gather you out of all countries, and bring you into your own land.
>
> *Ezekiel 36:24*

> But I will gather the remnant of My flock out of all countries where I have driven them, and bring them back to their folds; and they shall be fruitful and increase.
>
> *Jeremiah 23:3*

I was raised as a Reform Jew, which is the largest and most liberal branch of Judaism. Like most Jews, especially Reform Jews, I did not even consider reading the Bible. It was not on my radar screen or "to do" list. Like most Reform Jews I rarely went to services and did not practice Judaism.

While growing up, I do not recall ever meeting a Jew who seemed to have read *any* of the Bible much less studied it or followed it. Occasionally, I would meet a religious Jew, but all I saw in them was a fanatical adherence to monotonous, unnecessary rules and rituals. I would go to High Holiday services (*Rosh Hashanah* and *Yom Kippur*) and literally count the minutes until the service was over. My study of the prayer book consisted of calculating the number of pages that remained until the service would conclude—and it was always more than I thought I could easily endure. My favorite part of the service was when the rabbi told us to skip the next few pages.

I had no idea what I was reciting from the prayer book during services. I never quite knew what to do during the silent prayer time. "Uh, hello, God, it's me, Jim. If you are real, uh...please do the following things for me..." I think the rabbi told us to make it a silent prayer because he knew many of us had no idea what to pray and might totally embarrass ourselves if we prayed out loud. Even if one of my prayers had seemingly been "answered," I would have thought it simply a coincidence.

Like most Reform Jews, I left Judaism to the rabbis—the religious authorities. Who was I to question them? However, I don't recall any rabbi telling me the Hebrew Scriptures prophesied that the Messiah would come to redeem the Jewish people in approximately 32 CE. They never mentioned any of the 300+ prophecies concerning the Messiah in the Hebrew Scriptures much less that Yeshua had fulfilled them. They never mentioned that Yeshua can be found in countless passages in the Hebrew Scriptures. Perhaps no one had told them either.

My First Significant Encounters with Christians

After my college years at the University of Missouri at Columbia, before I started law school in 1975, I backpacked around Western Europe alone for three months. Despite some language barriers, it was not too challenging to figure out the European buses and trains.

However, before I arrived in Europe, I could not figure out how to get from LaGuardia Airport to Kennedy International Airport, both in New York. A discerning priest looked at me outside the airport and noted that I looked "lost." He put his arm on my shoulder and kindly said "Son, I am going where you are going. Let me show you the way." He hailed a taxi for us. We had a pleasant discussion along the way and he helped me get acclimated on my journey. To this day, I vividly remember that brief time with him and what a life-saver he was. But most notably I recall the peace and joy he had.

During my travels in Europe, I stayed at many Christian youth hostels. I was on a meager budget, and hostels were economical—about $2 or $3 a night. For that you got a noisy night's sleep on a lumpy musty mattress, in a smelly, crowded room, and a continental breakfast that was not worth a nickel, and tasted like one.

During my stays at the Christian youth hostels, I had a revelation—many of the people working at these hostels seemed to possess that same peace and joy as that priest in New York. They exuded love and warmth. Although relatively poor and facing other challenges in life, they seemed to be filled with more joy than I had ever experienced—and I was a healthy, up-and-coming lawyer from a caring family.

How did these people get that way? Why was I not like that? Instead I was always preoccupied and worried about things not being exactly as I thought they should be. As it says in the Messianic writings, they were provoking me to jealousy:

> But through their [the Jews] fall, to provoke them [the Jews] to jealousy, salvation has come to the Gentiles.
> *Romans 11:11*

I wanted the contentment these people had—the joy that captures the light of Messiah and brings revival to our souls. To my amazement, I have it today. Thank God!

One particularly memorable experience in Europe was my excursion to the Vatican. It seemed like a holy, tranquil place. I did not realize at the time that St. Peter's Cathedral at the Vatican was named after one of the Jewish disciples chosen by Yeshua. I decided to purchase an audio tour so I could learn about the cathedral's history, artwork, stained glass, and statuary. I opened the door to a booth with a sign on it that said "English," believing it was the place where I could hear the tour in my native language. To my surprise I had walked into a confessional booth—for people who spoke English. I quickly closed the door. *Oy vey,* I thought, what a place to do such a thing! I knew I should linger for a while and apologize to the priest. When the confession was over, I apologized, and the priest was extremely forgiving and understanding. I remember he said, "No harm done son." Whew!

More Encounters with Christians as I Commenced my Legal Career

In 1978, as I began my law career, I began to encounter anti-Semitism. Since I desired success, I decided that unless asked, I would simply not mention being Jewish, so as not to stifle my career. "Don't ask, don't tell" was my motto. Not many asked, and slowly I began to lose my identity as a Jew.

I also began to meet Christians. I was shocked to learn that many of them were very bright people who were not just blindly and naively following some religious doctrine. Some, in fact, were among the best attorneys in town.

About this time, I married Cathy, a kind and loving Catholic. Her family had that same peace and joy I had sensed in the priest in New York and at the Christian youth hostels in Europe. Cathy came from a large, loving extended family, and they all got along remarkably well. That amazed me; it seemed that their faith and trust in the Messiah was the source of this remarkable unity.

One of Cathy's sisters began to pass along books and pamphlets to me about God and the Bible. She also patiently responded to questions I posed challenging God and faith. These "Q&A" sessions began to chisel away at my hard heart piece by piece. God bless her and the rest of Cathy's family for their patience. A few years passed before I read any of the literature she had given me.

Eventually, as I began to inquire more, I discovered that many Christians had actually thought through these puzzling issues. Always an inquisitive sort who could make someone's chin drop to the ground with my probing questions, I challenged their beliefs—and they would patiently explain. To my surprise, it began to make sense. I could not believe my ears! Intelligent people had examined these issues of faith and found God and Yeshua to be real.

I vowed that one day I would read the Bible. My intention was that it would be an intellectual pursuit. Nonetheless, for years I never found the time. Instead, I allowed other matters to take precedence.

C.S. Lewis' Book, *Mere Christianity*

At the age of 37, I finally began to explore the Bible, but I did not start out by reading it. A concerned, loving person suggested that I read C.S. Lewis' classic *Mere Christianity*. I followed that advice and commenced my pursuit of learning about God, the Bible, and salvation.

C. S. Lewis was a brilliant, analytical man who had been an atheist. Setting out to disprove the Bible through extensive study and research, he instead became convinced it was true! Lewis' friend and colleague J.R.R. Tolkien, author of *The Hobbit* and *The Lord of the Rings*, was instrumental in opening his heart.

In *Mere Christianity*, C.S. Lewis thoroughly analyzes the world in which we live and logically explains why God must exist. He presents evidence for Yeshua's resurrection and God's promise of salvation (eternal life). Lewis meticulously lays out his thought process, analysis, and logic; it all made perfect sense. I found his logic to be irrefutable. It seemed to be an open and shut case. God does exist! He has to! I was beginning to be transformed...mentally. The evidence for the resurrection even seemed overwhelming. The veil that had prevented my mind from seeing these truths was finally being partially lifted, just as it is written:

> For I do not desire, brethren [fellow Jews], that you should be ignorant of this mystery, lest you should be wise in your own opinion, that blindness in part has happened to Israel until the fullness of the Gentiles has come in [i.e., initially most Jews will not recognize Yeshua as the Messiah].
>
> *Romans 11:25*

What were Lewis' arguments? I will briefly reiterate three of them.

1. Yeshua's followers would not be tortured and killed for a lie.

2. The tomb was empty.

3. It is documented that after His death Yeshua appeared to hundreds.

While reading *Mere Christianity,* my mind began to process the facts in a way I could understand them. A light was flickering!

Bill Gothard's Institute in Basic Life Principles

Reading *Mere Christianity* had piqued my curiosity. I desired to learn more. Next, I shocked my wife and others by attending a seminar called "The Institute in Basic Life Principles" (www.iblp.org). At his week-long seminar, Bill Gothard demonstrated repeatedly how the Bible offered simple solutions for life's problems. Life was not as complicated as I had tried to make it. For example, if we are in constant conflict and turmoil with our parents or children, it is quite likely we are not following the instructions in the Bible dealing with the parent-child relationship. Gothard listed example after example of how anxiety and discontentment are usually brought on by failing to follow God's gentle loving instructions. These instructions protect us much like an umbrella in the rain—until we step outside their covering.

One of the life-changing biblical rules Gothard illustrated was that God instructs us to forgive those who offend us. I frequently had ignored this rule and bore a grudge to convey to others not to even think about messing with me again. But what happened when I refused to forgive? *I* suffered. Why? Because bitterness can literally make us physically sick and can harm our bones:

> A merry heart does good, like medicine, but a broken
> spirit dries the bones.
>
> *Proverbs 17:22*

> When I kept silent, my bones grew old through my
> groaning all the day long.
>
> *Psalm 32:3*

When we hold on to bitterness, it is as if we drink a cup of poison that continues to infect our body and soul.

Similarly, when we offend someone and choose to ignore our misdeed, we quite likely will feel uneasy whenever we see that person. I have found that as soon as I apologize, repent, and ask for forgiveness, I receive mercy and am set free:

> He who covers his sins will not prosper, but whoever
> confesses and forsakes them will have mercy.
>
> *Proverbs 28:13*

In 1973, Dr. Karl Menninger, world-renowned psychologist and founder of the Menninger Foundation, acknowledged the healing that occurs when we simply receive and offer forgiveness. He concluded that if he could help his mental health patients simply receive and deliver forgiveness, 75% of them would be healed![115]

The Bill Gothard seminar radically ramped up my perspective on God and the Bible. I was becoming educated; the God-given principles of Scripture were making more and more sense. How could I have missed it all these years? The fog was lifting and my misconceptions were vanishing. My hardened heart toward God was softening. I hungered to learn more.

I was developing a peace as I learned that someone "upstairs" loved me unconditionally and was on my side. How liberating! I was not in this alone. It was no longer Jim versus the world. The Creator of the remarkable universe had loved me even before I was born and was watching over me:

> Before I formed you in the womb I knew you;
>
> *Jeremiah 1:5*

Messianic Judaism—What in the World is That?

Shortly after the Gothard seminar, my precious wife Cathy heard God's still, small voice speak to her heart and say we would be "Messianic Jews." At the time she did not even know what a Messianic Jew was, and neither did I! Cathy began to inquire and discovered that Messianic Jews are Jews who have found their Messiah.

A short while later, Cathy learned of a Messianic synagogue starting in our city—a place where Jews and Gentiles worshipped together. It seemed like a great compromise on an issue Cathy and I had been struggling with. Cathy was Catholic and I was Jewish and we had young children. The battle of my religion versus hers would be gone. At this point, I had been a lawyer for 14 years. Lawyers frequently try to settle a dispute by finding common ground that will satisfy both sides—a win-win situation. Messianic Judaism seemed like just that. Who had thought of this? What a simply awesome idea!

From the moment I walked in to my first Messianic gathering, I felt a tremendous peace. It was as if I had come home. The people were incredibly warm, loving, and caring. They had a peace and joy about them similar to that I had observed in the priest in New York, the Christians in the youth hostels in Europe, and the loving members of Cathy's family.

The music at the Messianic service touched my heart. I found it tremendously uplifting and full of life. It resonated within me in a powerful way and filled me with a peace I had never felt before. I later learned that as I sang worship songs, I would draw nearer to God and feel the joy and contentment that He desired for me. God was blessing me for following His instruction to praise Him with music and song:

> Come, let us sing for joy to the Lord; let us shout aloud
> to the Rock of our salvation. Let us come before Him
> with thanksgiving and extol Him with music and song.
> *Psalm 95:1–2 (NIV)*

For the first time in my life, I actually looked forward to going to services. There was music, dancing, joy, love, and fellowship—all filled with richness and depth. There were also revelatory and insightful teachings. I was being blessed immeasurably!

Today I frequently hear people share similar comments when they attend a Messianic service. They say things such as, "I felt so much love and unity at the congregation." Or "I can't put my finger on it but I felt at peace when I was there."

The Night I Finally Surrendered and Said "Yes" to God

On May 1, 1992, at a Friday night service, the Messianic rabbi honored Holocaust Remembrance Day (the anniversary of the liberation of the concentration camps after World War II). He played a video on the story of Rose Price, a holocaust survivor who accepted Yeshua as her Messiah after being released from the concentration camps.[116] Rose shared that upon her release from the camps, she was extremely angry and bitter at the Nazis and God for the anguish that had been inflicted upon her. She had undergone numerous surgeries over the years for the injuries she received in the camps and no longer believed in God.

After immigrating to the United States, Rose married Charlie Price and settled in Philadelphia to raise a family of four children. Rose's daughter and husband became followers of Yeshua. This caused great anguish and distress to Rose. They told her about Yeshua—that He loved her and wanted her to surrender her life to Him and to let God be the Lord of her life. After many arguments and much prayer, Rose accepted Yeshua as her Messiah, and her life was changed forever.[117]

A few years later, Rose felt that God wanted her to return to Germany and forgive the Nazis. She struggled and pleaded with God to no avail. He had a plan for Rose's life—to help deliver people from their separation from God. Of course God was not going to back down just because Rose did not understand this plan at the time.

While in Germany, Rose spoke to over 37,000 Germans about forgiveness. Rose struggled, but God gave her the grace to forgive the Nazis. As I had learned at the Bill Gothard seminar, by following God's instruction to forgive, Rose experienced blessing and healing. After forgiving the Nazis, her anger, bitterness, and unrest subsided. Surgeries were no longer necessary and she was set free from the bondage of bitterness and unforgiveness. The bitter poison was gone from her body. Hallelujah!

When Rose personally forgave individual Nazis, the guilt they had been carrying for decades lifted, and six of them came to her and repented. One of the Nazis had been a guard in a camp in which she had been imprisoned!

After presenting this Rose Price video, the Messianic Rabbi asked if anyone wanted to similarly be set free and let Yeshua into their heart. I raised my hand, thinking "Sure I *want* what Rose has. Who wouldn't?" I silently said a short prayer expressing my desire to know Yeshua as my Messiah. Bolts of lightening did not strike the ground. In fact, nothing seemed to change, but I now know that at that moment God had begun a work in me. My act of turning to God, and asking for His grace, enabled the veil that was blinding me from the truth to be lifted, just as was written by Rabbi Saul of Tarsus (Paul):

> But even to this day, when Moses is read, a veil lies on
> their heart. Nevertheless when one turns to the Lord,
> the veil is taken away.
>
> *2 Corinthians 3:15–16*

Previously, I had often used swear words around men. Starting the very next day, I had a new strong conviction that cursing was wrong. Curse words would come to my lips, but I could not utter them. The words would simply stop at my lips! I had not consciously made a decision to stop cursing. I didn't even have a desire to stop. I just stopped. I now know that this was God beginning to purify me.

Over the next few weeks, my wife Cathy would periodically ask me if I had accepted Yeshua yet, and my response was always "Not yet, but I still *want* to know Him." As I look back, I am astonished I did not recognize that God had done a miracle by convicting me of cursing.

A short while later, our rabbi scheduled a *t'vilah* ceremony (water immersion or baptism) and I signed up for it. I thought this would just be another step in the process. On the way to the immersion, Cathy pointed out to me that I would have to publicly declare my acceptance of Yeshua as the Son of God who died for my sins. I was shocked! *Oy vey!* I didn't know I would have to do *that*. When I got out of the car, I nervously paced back and forth as I pondered what to do. I thought of backing out, but our rabbi had printed a flyer with the names of those participating in the water immersion, and I was on it. If I backed out, it would be terribly embarrassing. "Ladies and gentleman, Jim has decided that you guys are insane, that he does not believe what you believe, and has chickened out." So I decided to go through with it. After making that decision, my heart changed, and I was finally able to accept Yeshua.

Accompanied by the rabbi and many observers, I stood waist deep in a lake, proclaimed my faith in Yeshua, and immersed my entire body. At that moment I was spiritually cleansed in the waters of the *t'vilah*. When I came out of the water, it felt as if I jumped five feet in the air—I hadn't but it was that exhilarating. Cathy was re-immersed that day as well, and we embraced soaking wet. It was a glorious day and is the day I became a follower of Yeshua. I felt like a new person! I was a new creation! I knew Yeshua had transformed me. As He promised:

> Whoever confesses Me before men, him I will also
> confess before My father who is in heaven.
> *Matthew 10:32*

Since that day, God has radically changed my life, Cathy's life, and the lives of our children. God has graciously and lovingly continued to refine and purify me, little by little, over the last 16 years. Am I perfect? By no means! Do I know that I am forgiven for my sins? Absolutely! Do I know who to turn to during turbulent times and who to thank when things go well? Definitely!

Now I understand that Yeshua's sacrificial death was the final *Yom Kippur* sacrifice that provided redemption and forgiveness for all people! He was the perfect, unblemished Passover lamb spoken of in the Torah in the Book of Exodus, the one who was slain as a sacrifice for us. His blood protects us and delivers us from a spiritual death just as blood on their doorposts protected the Israelites from a physical death in Egypt at the time of Moses *(Exodus 12)*. Just as the *Afikomen* (middle *matzah*) is broken on Passover, wrapped in a cloth, and hidden, only to be discovered later on (for which the discoverer receives a reward), Yeshua was broken, wrapped in a burial cloth, and sealed in a tomb. Whoever finds Him receives an eternal reward.

Yeshua as Lord

Yeshua is the ultimate role model, the One who will neither leave you nor forsake you. Yeshua went before you and paid the price for your sins, so that you could be found "not guilty" by reason of His redemption, His sacrifice, and His love for us. What a mighty deliverer He is! Throw yourself upon the mercy of the heavenly court, and He will give you peace and free you from sin and guilt. Yeshua wants to bring peace to your heart.

How many of you who have rejected Yeshua have never read the Messianic writings? I urge you to read them and receive their message of God's love. I heard a leading Reform rabbi encourage all Jewish people to read the Messianic writings and *Isaiah 53*. This amazing chapter, found in the Hebrew Scriptures, is contained in Appendix B of this book. It prophesies the Messiah as the suffering servant; Yeshua's life, crucifixion, and death are foretold in this compelling prophecy written over 700 years before His birth.

I have heard people say that they believe Yeshua lived and had many followers, but do not believe all that is written about Him in the Bible. That is, they do not believe He is the Son of God who performed miracles, came to die for the sins of the world, and will come again. To me, the Bible is either true or not. There is no middle ground. If we believe parts of it—the descriptions of the lives of Abraham, Moses, and King David—and accept portions of the Yeshua accounts, then it would follow that the rest is credible as well, especially in light of the evidence presented in Chapter 3.

If you believe that Yeshua is the prophesied Messiah, wouldn't you want to serve Him with all your heart, soul, mind, and strength? Imagine saying, "I believe Superman is in the next room, but I am going to just go about my business." We would not say that. We would want to get to know him. We would want to listen and talk to him and be by his side.

Shouldn't it be the same with God? If you believe He exists and is the Creator of the finely-tuned universe and our incredibly intricate bodies, then I challenge you to learn more about Him, to read more about Him, to talk to Him (in prayer), and to follow His instructions. All you have to do is surrender to Him and recognize and trust His supernatural abilities—the same ones that created the universe and formed human life from the dust of the earth. The universe is God's creation, and it seems clear that He made it for your enjoyment and mine. His works are worthy of our highest praise.

Conclusion

I now clearly see the other side to the arguments I previously had made against God, Yeshua, and the Bible. I hope this book has made you ponder these same issues. Perhaps your heart has been softened. If it hasn't, then I would urge you to put this book back on the shelf and read it again at another time, or perhaps read another book examining the evidence for God, the Bible, and Yeshua. God knows the time in your life when it is best for you to meet Him. My wife and I had to cancel our first date due to a scheduling conflict. I did not call her again for a year. We have since learned that had we started dating a year earlier, it would not have been the right time, and we may have never ended up together.

My prayer is that right now is the time for you to reach out to God. Appendix A lists books, music, and other resources that might assist you. Simply examine the ones that seem most appropriate for you.

I will close with an inquiry: Do you have assurance that you will spend eternity in heaven? If you have any doubts, I urge you to take a step of faith and say the following prayer with an open heart and a sincere desire to know God. It is the most important thing you will ever do.

God of Abraham, Isaac, and Jacob, I thank you that you are willing to carry my burdens and to fill my heart abundantly with peace. I invite you into my life to be my Lord and Savior. I recognize that I have done wrong in Your sight. I repent for my sins and ask for Your forgiveness.

> *Thank you that you are a forgiving merciful God. I*
> *accept Your Son, Messiah Yeshua, into my heart and life.*
> *I believe Yeshua rose from the dead and has paid the*
> *price for my sins, which are now covered by His blood.*
> *I invite Your Spirit to dwell within me and to be my*
> *comforter and instructor all the days of my life. I*
> *pray these things in the name of Yeshua. Thank you,*
> *God, for this wonderful gift of salvation that You prom-*
> *ised and that I have now received through my Messiah.*

If you said this prayer, hallelujah! You are a new creation!

> Therefore, if anyone is united with the Messiah, he is
> a new creation—the old has passed; look, what has
> come is fresh and new!
>
> *2 Corinthians 5:17 (CJB)*

May your life be forever changed. May I also suggest that you consider the following to assist you with your walk with God:

Read the Bible Daily

Try to read the Bible for at least 10 minutes a day. It is spiritual food and light. You do not have to read it in the order it is written, since it is not in chronological order. You may wish to start with the gospels (Matthew, Mark, Luke, and John), Psalms, or Proverbs. Find a translation you are comfortable with, perhaps without all the "thees" and "thous." A particular translation may be better suited for you, so look at several before digging in. Pray before you read something such as: "God, I love you. You are awesome! Please illuminate Your Word to me and touch my heart and life in a powerful way." You can find Bible study guides in bookstores or online. Recognize that you may not understand everything at first but will grow in your knowledge of God through His Word. It is amazing how a single verse at the right moment can change your life, and the same verses can have different meanings at different times in your life.

Apply What You Read

Act upon what the Bible instructs you to do. Forgive your enemies, go the extra mile, and love your neighbor as yourself. Rejoice that you know Him!

Pray Every Day

Pray throughout the day. It need not be a ritual. It does not have to be eloquent. Prayer is simply communicating and spending time with God. Try to pray from your heart. Cry out to Him either verbally or silently. Share your burdens and your heart with Him. Praise Him for the things He has done. Develop a relationship with Him. He may speak to you in a way that almost seems like a thought—that is His still, small voice that you will come to recognize. But remember, if this "voice" is inconsistent with what you read in the Bible, it is not from God.

Find Fellowship

Locate a Messianic Congregation or church in your area (preferably one that recognizes the significance of Israel today and the Jewish roots of the faith), so you can fellowship with other Believers in the Messiah. For a directory of Messianic Congregations in your area, check the *Yellow Pages* under "Synagogues" or go online. See www.iamcs.org, www.umjc.org or www.messianictimes.com/messianicdirectory.php.[118]

* * *

If you are not ready to say the above-mentioned prayer, why not simply tell God you sincerely want to know the truth, and ask Him to reveal Himself to you? As previously noted, God is faithful and promises that if you seek Him with all your heart you will find Him:

> …you will seek Me and find Me, when you search for
> Me with all your heart.
> > *Jeremiah 29:13*

Abundant blessings to you all!

Appendix A

Resources
Books to Help Establish Your Faith

I Have a Friend Who is Jewish, Do You?
Don Goldstein
A short, easy-to-read book that provides evidence of the existence of God, the validity of the Bible, and Messiahship of Yeshua
813-655-4220
www.prophecyrevealed.com (read for free on line or order)

Messianic Answer Book (available in English and Russian)
Sam Nadler
Answers questions about the Messiah
704-362-1927
www.wordofmessiah.org

Answering Jewish Objections to Jesus (Parts 1, 2, 3, 4)
Michael L. Brown
Thorough and scholarly responses to the most common objections to faith in Yeshua
800-410-7367
www.messianicjewish.net

They Thought for Themselves
Sid Roth
Testimonies of Jewish Believers from many walks of life
800-548-1918
www.sidroth.org

Born a Jew...Die a Jew
Yohanna Chernoff
Wife of the late Rabbi Martin Chernoff, pioneer of modern Messianic Judaism, Yohanna shares the history of the revival of the late 20th century
215-477-2706
www.kesherministries.org; www.amazon.com

Yeshua the Messiah
Rabbi David Chernoff
Basic discussion of the messiahship of Yeshua from a Messianic rabbi
215-477-2706
www.kesherministries.org

Mere Christianity
C.S. Lewis
Evidence of the existence of God, the validity of the Bible, and that Yeshua is the Messiah
909-793-0949
www.amazon.com

Ready With an Answer
John Ankerburg and John Weldon
Discussion on the authenticity of Scripture and belief in Yeshua
800-805-3030
www.amazon.com

Evidence That Demands a Verdict
Josh McDowell
Detailed evidence of the existence of God and the Bible's authenticity
866-252-5424
www.amazon.com

The Stones Cry Out
Randall Price
Archaeological discoveries that verify the history recorded in the Bible
866-604-7322
www.amazon.com

Books for Building Your Faith

Messianic Daily Devotional
Kevin Geoffrey
Rich daily devotional; short daily scripture and two pages of commentary
888-321-PWMI (7964)
www.messiahwordministries.com

Following Yeshua (available in English and Russian)
Growing in Messiah (available in English and Russian)
Sam Nadler
Discipleship for new and maturing believers
704-362-1927
www.wordofmessiah.org

God's Appointed Times
Barney Kasdan
Scriptural and traditional study of the biblical festivals and their fulfillment in Yeshua
800-773-6574
www.messianicjewish.net

God's Appointed Customs
Barney Kasdan
Scriptural and traditional study of Jewish customs and their fulfillment in Yeshua
800-773-6574
www.messianicjewish.net

Growing to Maturity
Daniel C. Juster
Discipling overview of Messianic Jewish life
800-692-8652
www.messianicjewish.net

You Bring the Bagels, I'll Bring the Gospel
Barry Rubin
An insightful book to help understand how to share the gospel
800-773-6574
www.messianicjewish.net

Complete Jewish Bible
David Stern, translator
Scriptures translated by a Jewish Bible scholar living in Israel
800-773-6574
www.messianicjewish.net

Jewish New Testament and Commentary
David Stern
Commentary elucidating the Jewishness of the New Testament
800-773-6574
www.messianicjewish.net

Our Father Abraham
Marvin Wilson
Discusses Jewish roots of the Christian faith
800-773-6574
www.messianicjewish.net

Epicenter
Joel Rosenberg
New York Times bestseller. A journey through biblical prophecy
800-773-6574
www.messianicjewish.net

Halley's Bible Handbook
Henry H. Halley
Bestselling Bible study guide
800-247-4784
www.amazon.com

Websites and Ministries

Messianic Jewish Resources
Carries many of the books mentioned above, and others, plus videos
and CDs
800-410-7367
www.messianicjewish.net

The Galilee Experience
Carries numerous books, videos, and CDs
888-838-7928
www.thegalileeexperience.com

Hope of the World
Free one-minute daily devotional and free gifts
973-472-4978
www.hopeoftheworld.com

Perfect Word Ministry
Messianic website with daily devotional, books, and literature
888-321-PWMI (7964)
www.perfect-word.org

Tikkun Ministry
Rich free monthly newsletter from Israel
301-977-3515
www.tikkunministries.org

Messianic Jewish Alliance of America
Resource for Messianic conferences, humanitarian programs, and more
800-225-MJAA (6522)
www.mjaa.org

Union of Messianic Jewish Congregations
Resource for Messianic conferences, humanitarian programs, and more
800-692-8652
www.umjc.org

Jewish Jewels
Insightful free monthly newsletter and other resources
800-293-7482
www.jewishjewels.org

Road to Jerusalem
Ministry of peace and reconciliation between Jews and Gentiles
303-991-0550
www.roadtojerusalem.org

Messianic Music

Messianic Jewish Resources
800-410-7367
www.messianicjewish.net

Galilee of the Nations
877-327-7306
www.galileeofthenations.com

Paul Wilbur
904-565-9909
www.wilburministries.com

Joel Chernoff/Lamb
610-338-0451
www.lambmessianicmusic.com

Marty Goetz
616-661-4564
www.martygoetz.com

Ted Pearce
(214) 693 6464
www.tedpearce.com

Kathy Shooster
(215) 477-2706
www.kathyshooster.com

Zemer Levav
877-327-7306
www.zemerlevav.org

Appendix B

Isaiah 53

From the Hebrew Scriptures, written in approximately 700 BCE

"Who has believed our message and to whom has the arm of the Lord been revealed? He grew up before him like a tender shoot, and like a root out of dry ground. He had no beauty or majesty to attract us to him, nothing in his appearance that we should desire him. He was despised and rejected by men, a man of sorrows, and familiar with suffering. Like one from whom men hide their faces he was despised, and we esteemed him not.

"Surely he took up our infirmities and carried our sorrows, yet we considered him stricken by God, smitten by him, and afflicted. But he was pierced for our transgressions, he was crushed for our iniquities; the punishment that brought us peace was upon him, and by his wounds we are healed. We all, like sheep, have gone astray, each of us has turned to his own way; and the Lord has laid on him the iniquity of us all. He was oppressed and afflicted, yet he did not open his mouth [he did not answer his accusers]; he was led like a lamb to the slaughter, and as a sheep before her shearers is silent, so he did not open his mouth. By oppression and judgment he was taken away. And who can speak of his descendants? For he was cut off from the land of the living; for the transgression of my people he was stricken. He was assigned a grave with the wicked, and with the rich in his death, though he had done no violence, nor was any deceit in his mouth.

"Yet it was the Lord's will to crush him and cause him to suffer, and though the Lord makes his life a guilt offering, he will see his offspring and prolong his days, and the will of the Lord will prosper in his hand. After the suffering of his soul, he will see the light of life and be satisfied; by his knowledge my righteous servant will justify many, and he will bear their iniquities. Therefore I will give him a portion among the great, and he will divide the spoils with the strong, because he poured out his life unto death, and was numbered with the transgressors. For he bore the sin of many, and made intercession for the transgressors." *(NIV)*

Comment

Some rabbis today say that the "he" in this passage is referring to Israel. To this I have three brief responses:

1. Focus on these sentences contained in the first paragraph of *Isaiah 53* above:

   > *He* was despised and rejected by men, a man of sorrows, and familiar with suffering. Like one from whom men hide their faces *he* was despised, and *we* esteemed him not.

   Here the "we" clearly refers to Israel. So the "he" cannot also refer to the Israel. The "he" must refer to someone else and the only plausible explanation is that "he" refers to the Messiah. Also, in *Isaiah 52*, Isaiah refers to Israel as "Zion," not "he."

2. It says "he had done no violence" yet we know Israel has done violence throughout its many wars.

3.   It says "he poured out his life unto death" but we know that Israel is a viable nation.

Read *Isaiah 53* and decide for yourself. It does not seem even remotely to refer to Israel.

An Orthodox rabbi once told me *Isaiah 53* referred to the Messiah but that the Jewish people are waiting for a King (Son of David) as their Messiah, not a Suffering Servant (Son of Joseph) to which this passage refers. A reading of the Hebrew Scriptures seems to refer to the Messiah as both a Suffering Servant and King: "They will look on me, the one they have pierced…" *(Zechariah 12:10, NIV);* "…he shall be a priest upon his throne" *(Zechariah 6:13, NIV).* It seems implausible that He would come one time as both a Suffering Servant and King. Could it be that the Messiah comes once as a Suffering Servant, as He did 2,000 years ago, and later to reign as a King?

Endnotes

1   Isaacson, Walter. "In Search of The Real Bill Gates." *Time,* October 20, 2005.

2   McCabe, Stephen and Stan Goldman. *Hand, Wrist and Arm Sourcebook.* Chicago: NTC Contemporary, 2000.

3   MacHale, Des. *Wisdom.* London: Prion Books, Ltd., 2002.

4   *The Journal of Comparative Neurology* 238, Issue 1 (2004): 92–100; Wadhwa, S. and V. Bijlani. Developing human optic nerve in prenatal period changes in the numbers of retinal axons. Volume 35, Issue 1, 11–16 (1987); Giglio, Louie. *How Great is Our God* DVD. www.268generation.com.

5   Darwin, Charles. *Origin of Species by Means of Natural Selection.* London: J.M. Dent & Sons Ltd., 1971,167; Eliot, Charles W., editor. *The Harvard Classics.* New York: P.F. Collier & Son Company, 1909, Vol. 11, 190.

6   Myers, David G. *Psychology.* New York: Worth Publishers, 2007, 230.

7   Farabee, M.J. *The Digestive System, Online Biology Book.* Avondale, 1996: Maricopa Community College. http://www.emc.maricopa.edu/faculty/farabee/BIOBK/BioBookTOC.html.

8   Freitas, Robert A. *Nanomedicine. Volume I: Basic Capabilities.* Georgetown: Landes Bioscience,1999, section 8.51.; Richards, Lawrence O. *It Couldn't Just Happen.* Nashville: Thomas Nelson, Inc.,1986; The Nobel Prize in Physiology or Medicine 2001 Press Release, October 8, 2001, 1; Phillips, Roger E. *The Heart and the Circulatory System.* Burlington: Carolina Biological Supply Company.

9   Cavalli-Sforza, L. Luca. "How can one study individual variation for 3 billion nucleotides of the human genome?" *American Journal of Human Genetics,* April 1990, 649–651.

10   Karton, Carol. *Making the Grade: Everything Your 6th Grader Needs to Know.* Hauppauge: Barron's Educational Services, Inc., 2004; *How Great is Our God* DVD.

11   Campbell, Mary K. and Shawn O. Farrell. *Biochemistry.* Florence: Thomson Brooks/Cole, 2006.

12   Shormann, David E. *The Exchange of Truth.* Lincoln: iUniverse, 2007.

13   *Merriam-Webster On Line Dictionary; Joy Magazine* article by Dr. Peter Hammond, Issue 13–2007; Google Images; *How Great is Our God* DVD.

14   *Psychology,* 199.

15   *Psychology,* 199–231.

16   *Psychology,* 217.

17   *Psychology,* 233 and 250.

18   Darwin, Charles. *The Origin of Species.* New York: Random House, Modern Library Edition, 1993, 184.

19   *It Couldn't Just Happen,* 114.

20   DeMar, Gary. "My Introductory Comments at the Dayton to Dothon Creation to Evolution Debate," *The American Vision,* November 28, 2007; "A Scientific Dissent for Darwinisim." *Biblical Worldview Magazine,* January/February 2008, 11; Staff. "Doubts Over Evolution Mount with Over 300 Scientists Expressing Skepticism with Central Tenet of Darwin's Theory," *Discovery Institute,* April 1, 2004.

21   DeMar, Gary. "My Introductory Comments at the Dayton to Dothon Creation to Evolution Debate," *The American Vision,*

November 28, 2007; "Physicians and Surgeons for Scientific Integrity." *Biblical Worldview Magazine*, January/February 2008, 11.

22 *Origin of Species by Means of Natural Selection.* 2; "John Lofton's Journal," (*The Washington Times,* February 8, 1984); Snelling, Andrew. *The Revised Quotebook.* Brisbane: Creation Science Foundation, 1990, 3.

23 *Notre Dame Magazine.* Winter 2005–06.

24 Banks, Stephen L. "Asklepios." *Annals of Internal Medicine,* August 1, 1996, Volume 125, Issue 3, 253; Chicago: *Encyclopedia Britannica.*

25 Commager, Henry Steele and Richard B. Morris. *Spirit of Seventy-Six.* New York: The Bobbs-Merrill Co., Inc. 1958; Marshall, Peter and David Manuel. *The Glory of America.* Bloomington: Garborg's Heart'N Home, Inc., 1991.

26 Anderson, Joan Wester. *Guardian Angels: True Stories of Answered Prayer;* posted at the George Washington Carver National Monument near Diamond, Missouri, 129.

27 Unanimous declaration of the original 13 states of America, July 4, 1776.

28 Mackie, Glen. "To See the Universe in a Grain of Taranaki Sand." *North and South* Magazine, May 1999.

29 *How Great is Our God* DVD.

30 Davies, Paul. *The Cosmic Blueprint: New Discoveries in Nature's Ability to Order the Universe.* New York: Touchstone Books, 1989, 203.

31 Tiner, J.H. *Louis Pasteur—Founder of Modern Medicine.* Milford: Mott Media, 1990, 75.

32 Kings, military leaders, peasants, philosophers, fishermen, tax collectors, poets, musicians, scholars, and shepherds. Note: Some believe that Luke was not Jewish.

33 Twain, Mark. *The Innocents Abroad.* American Publishing, 1869.

34 *CNBC European Business News* by Boyd Farrow (November 2007).

35 Fedler, John. *Focus on Israel: Israel's Agriculture in the 21st Century.* Israel Ministry of Foreign Affairs, December 24, 2002.

36 *Focus on Israel: Israel's Agriculture in the 21st Century,* December 24, 2002.

[37] Price, Randall. *The Stones Cry Out*. Eugene: Harvest House Publishers, 1997, 323; Glueck, Nelson. *Rivers in the Desert: A History of the Negev*. New York: Farrar, Strauss and Cudahy, 1959, 31 and 136.

[38] *The Stones Cry Out*.

[39] Lefkovits, Etgar. "Archeologist find 2nd Temple Quary." *Jerusalem Post*, September 23, 2007, Israel section, Online edition.

[40] *Nature News Service*. Macmillan Magazines Ltd, September 11, 2003.

[41] Wood, Bryant G. "The Discovery of the Sin Cities of Sodom and Gomorrah." *Bible and Spade*, Summer 1999.

[42] Meadville: *Allegheny College Alumni Bulletin*, Fall 1971.

[43] *The Stones Cry Out*, 235–237.

[44] *The Stones Cry Out*, 102–104.

[45] *The Stones Cry Out*, 165–174; interview with Bryant Wood, New Orleans, November 1996; Wilford, John. "Archaeologists say evidence of House of David found." *Dallas Morning News*, August 6, 1993.

[46] Garstang, John. *The Foundations of Bible History; Joshua, Judges*. London: Constable, 1931, 146.

[47] *The Stones Cry Out*, 324–325; Albright, W.F. *The Archaeology of Palestine*. London: Penguin Books, 1954, 128.

[48] Agard, Margaret. *Historical Proofs of the Bible*.

[49] *The Stones Cry Out*, p. 277.

[50] Staff writer. "Another Earthquake hits Israel." *Israel Today*, November 25, 2007.

[51] Ambraseyes, N. "Historical Earthquakes In Jerusalem." *Journal of Seismology*, Volume 9, number 2, July 2005.

[52] McMillen, S.I. *None of These Diseases*. Grand Rapids: Fleming H. Revell, 1984, 93; Korzybski, Alfred. *Sanity and Science*. Spring Valley: Feldheim Publishers.

[53] *Sanity and Science*.

[54] Cook, G.C. *Outbreak of trichinosis (trichiniasis) contracted in London in 1879*. Postgrad Med J 2001 Jan; 77(903): 62–3.

[55] Weinberg, Winkler G. *No Germs Allowed: How to Avoid Infectious Diseases at Home and On the Road*. Piscataway: Rutgers University Press, 1952.

56 Yancey, Philip, *What's So Amazing About Grace?* Grand Rapids: Zondervan, 1997, 149.

57 Shormann, David E. *The Exchange of Truth.* Bloomington: iUniverse, Inc., 2007, chapter 1.

58 Morris, Henry H. Men of Science—*Men of God. El Cajon:* Master Books, 1988, 23–26; Wilmington, Harold. *Wlimington's Guide to the Bible.* Wheaton: Tyndale House Publishers, Inc., 1981, 797.

59 Eidsmoe, John. *Christianity and the Constitution—The Faith of Our Founding Fathers.* Grand Rapids: Baker Book House, *A Mott Media Book,* 1987, 6th printing, 1993, 48.

60 *Wilmington's Guide to the Bible,* 797.

61 Federer, William J. *America's God and Country Encyclopedia of Quotations.* St. Louis: Amerisearch, 1996, 660; *Wilmington's Guide to the Bible,* 796.

62 *Wilmington's Guide to the Bible,* 796.

63 *Wilmington's Guide to the Bible,* 796.

64 Wampler, Dee. *The Myth of the Separation Between Church and State.* Enumclaw: Wine Press Publishing, 2003,124; Wilmington's Guide to the Bible, 796.

65 *Wilmington's Guide to the Bible,* 796.

66 *Wilmington's Guide to the Bible,* 796.

67 Gipp, Samuel C. *For His Pleasure.* Massillon: Friend To Church Ministries.

68 *America's God and Country Encyclopedia of Quotations,* 676.

69 *America's God and Country Encyclopedia of Quotations,* 289.

70 Federer, William J. *What Every American Needs to Know About the Qur'an-a History of Islam & the United States,* 235 and 257.

71 Filardo, Sonia. *The Truth Will Set You Free! It Will Transform You!* Las Vegas: The Truth Factor, 2005, 4. http://www.thetruthfactor.com/table_of_contents.htm.

72 McCartney, Clarence Edward. *Lincoln and the Bible.* New York: Abington-Cokesbury Press, 1949, 35.

73 *Spirit of Seventy-Six; The Glory of America.*

74 *Kansas City Star,* July 7, 2007, A4; *Parade,* July 29, 2007, 4.

75 Drosnin, Michael. *Citizen Hughes.* New York: Holt, Rinehart and

Winston, 1985, 49; Ortberg, John. *When the Game is Over It All Goes Back in the Box*. Grand Rapids: Zondervan, 2007, 190.

[76] Seligman, Martin. *Authentic Happiness*. New York: Free Press, 2002, 186.

[77] *When the Game is Over It All Goes Back in the Box*, 195.

[78] *When the Game is Over It All Goes Back in the Box*, 197.

[79] Throughout this chapter I have compared the translations I have provided with the translations offered by the Jewish Publication Society (JPS) and have found them to be very similar to each other. Sometimes the verse numbers vary slightly. Feel free to compare them for yourself at www.mechon-mamre.org/e/et/et0.htm. I have used the NIV translation when other translations capitalize pronouns and other words.

[80] *Babylonian Talmud, Soncino version*, Yoma 39b; Neusner, Jacob. *Jerusalem Talmud, The Yerushalmi*, 156–157.

[81] Again, some believe Luke was not Jewish.

[82] Jamie Cowen, President Union of Messianic Jewish Congregations (June 18, 2008).

[83] McGirk-Ariel, Tim. "Israel's Messianic Jews under Attack." *Time*, June 6, 2008.

[84] Youtube. "Messianic Jews Worshipping Yeshua (Jesus)." http://www.youtube.com/watch?v=3sEBAldf4L0.

[85] *Columbia Encyclopedia*. 6th ed, 2001.

[86] This revelation is discussed in Don Goldstein's book *I Have a Friend Who is Jewish, Do You?* a 70-page, easy-to-read book which provides evidence for God, the Bible, and the Messiahship of Yeshua. It can be read for free on line (prophecyrevealed.com) or purchased for under $10.

[87] Edwards, William D., Wesley J. Gabel and Floyd E. Hosmer. *On the Physical Death of Jesus Christ. Journal of American Medical Association*, 1986, 256:1455–1463, March 21; Davis, Truman C. *The Crucifixion of Jesus*. Mesa: Arizona Medicine, March 1965.

[88] Barney Fife was a bumbling deputy, portrayed by the late actor/comedian Don Knotts, on *The Andy Griffith Show* which originally aired in the '60s.

89 Maier, Paul L. *In Fullness of Time: A Historian Looks at Christmas, Easter, and the Early Church.* Grand Rapids: Kregel, 1998, 203.

90 Ankerberg, John and John Weldon. *The Evidence for the Resurrection of Jesus Christ, Part 2:* "Could the Evidence Stand Cross-Examination in a Modern Court of Law?" Chattanooga: Ankerberg and Burroughs.

91 *In Fullness of Time: A Historian Looks at Christmas, Easter, and the Early Church,* 203.

92 Green, Michael. *ManAlive!* Chicago: InterVarsity Christian Fellowship, 1969, 54.

93 Smith, Wilbur. *Therefore Stand: Christian Apologetics.* Grand Rapids: Baker Book House, 1974, 54.

94 *America's God and Country Encyclopedia of Quotations.*

95 "Our Christian Heritage," *Letter from Plymouth Rock,* 5.

96 McDowell, Stephen and Mark Beliles. *The Providential Perspective.* Charlottesville: The Providence Foundation, January 1994, 6.

97 *Halley's Bible Handbook.* Grand Rapids: Zondervan Publishing House, 1965, 19.

98 Bartlett, John. *Bartlett's Familiar Quotations.* Boston: Little, Brown and Company, 1855, 1980, 300.

99 Columbus, Christopher. *The Book of Prophecies.* Berkeley: University of California Press, June 21, 1997.

100 In October 2007 researchers at the University of Missouri at Columbia found that red wine defends against cardiovascular disease and tumors, and when combined with grape juice can help protect from common food borne disease. Red wine has anti-microbial properties that defend against food-borne pathogens and don't harm useful bacteria. *Kansas City Star.* October 12, 2007, B1.

101 Again, some feel Luke was not Jewish.

102 *Romans 2:26–29.*

103 Kac, Arthur. *The Messiahship of Jesus: Are Jews Changing Their Attitude Toward Jesus?* Grand Rapids: Baker Book House, revised edition, 1986; Viereck, George Sylvester. "What Life Means to Einstein." *The Saturday Evening Post,* October 26, 1929.

104 *The Messiahship of Jesus: Are Jews Changing Their Attitude Toward Jesus?*

105 Lapide, Pinchas. *The Resurrection of Jesus: A Jewish Perspective.* Minneapolis: Augsburg Publishing House,1983.

106 *The Messiahship of Jesus: Are Jews Changing Their Attitude Toward Jesus?;* "Three Talks on Judaism," translated by Paul Levertoff, "Jewish Opinions About Jesus," *Der Weg* 7 no. 1 (January–February, 1933).

107 *The Messiahship of Jesus: Are Jews Changing Their Attitude Toward Jesus?*

108 *The Messiahship of Jesus: Are Jews Changing Their Attitude Toward Jesus?*

109 Disraeli, Benjamin. *Lord George Bentinck: A Political Biography* (written in 1852) published by Archibald, Constable & Co. Ltd., London 1905, p. 330.

110 Rabbi Cohn's journey to faith in Yeshua is told in *To An Ancient People, The Autobiography of Rabbi Leopold Cohn.* Rabbi Cohn was born into an Orthodox family in 1862. He was a student of the Talmud (oral law recorded in ancient books which contain Jewish law, customs and history).

111 Brown, Michael L. *Answering Jewish Objections to Jesus.* Grand Rapids: Baker book House, 2000, 42.

112 Van Biema, David. "What's Next 2008." *Time,* March 12, 2008.

113 Gillet, Lev. *Communion in the Messiah: Studies in the Relationship Between Judaism and Christianity.* Cambridge: James Clarke & Co., 2002, 206; Einspruch, Henry. *Raisins and Almonds.* Baltimore: The Lewis and Harriet Lederer Foundation, 1967.

114 Van Biema, David, "The Case for Teaching the Bible." *Time,* March 22, 2007.

115 *Today In the Word,* March 1989, 8.

116 See www.rosepriceministries.org.

117 For a video entitled *Survivor Stories* on six Holocaust survivors who accepted Yeshua, see www.jewsforjesus.org or call 800-MESSIAH or 415-864-2600.

118 Most of these suggestions are taken from Jonathan Cahn's teaching tape, *First Steps,* which can be obtained by contacting Hope of the World (www.hopeoftheworld.com), Box 1111, Lodi, New Jersey 07644; phone: 973-472-4978.